A Voice in the Wilderness,
volume 5

The Sound of an Abundance of Rain

Dalen Garris

This is a work of history. Historical individuals and places and events are mentioned.

Copyright © 2020 by Dalen Garris

*Published by Revivalfire Ministries
Cover design by Kevin Haislip
Cover photo by*

ISBN 13: 978-1-7342213-5-0

*All rights reserved.
No part of this book may be used or reproduced in any manner whatsoever, without written permission, except in the case of brief quotations embodied in critical articles and reviews, as provided by U.S. Copyright Law.*

All Scripture is from the King James Version

*For information, address
dale@revivalfire.org*

First paperback printing December, 2020

Printed in the United States of America

Rev.2.1

Table of Contents

The Sound of an Abundance of Rain	1
No Burger King Salvation	4
Jerusalem	7
Excuse	11
Sodomites	14
Charley	17
Draw Me	20
Guesswork	23
Reading	28
Fruit of Righteousness	31
James, Peter, & John	34
Dross	38
Ireland	42
Chiropractor's Daughter	46
Plumbline is set	50
Kingdom of God Within	54
Your Name is Written There!	57
Letter from Chris	60
One More Night with the Frogs	65
One Thing	68
I'm Back	71

Gideon's Call	74
False Revival	78
Sure of Salvation	81
Where's the Beef?	83
Jacob's Staff	86
Prepared Messages	89
Touch the Cross	92
Meaningless Hope	95
Desired to Make One Wise	98
Kids	100
Debate	103
Progression	105
Squirrel	108
Balance	110
The Feast	113
Decision	116
Two Streams	119
Butcher in Kenya	123
The Old Prophet	127
About the Author	130

The Sound of an Abundance of Rain

"And Elijah said unto Ahab, Get thee up, eat and drink; for there is a sound of abundance of rain." I Kings 18:41

Last night, as we were in a prayer meeting of saints crying out for a fresh new move of God, the Lord opened my ears to hear what Elijah heard.

The events concerning Elijah's ministry have deep significance for these last days. From the time when he first presents himself to Ahab and declares a drought until the time when he is chased into the desert by Jezebel's persecution, we see a picture of how end-time events will unfold.

In a time of seeming great prosperity for backslidden Israel, Elijah's prophetic word of a coming drought seemed absurd. The judgments of God seemed far away from the lush green fields and prosperity that was all around. Life was good, and no one expected it to change.

And out of nowhere comes this hairy man that no one has heard of and stands right in the face of the king to declare something that, on the surface, seems laughable. Who was this unknown peasant with an outrageous attitude to rebuke the king himself right in the middle of the king's court?

But three and a half years later, no one was laughing.

We have gone through several years of spiritual drought. Prophets of God – <u>real</u> prophets of God – have warned us, but no one was listening. On the contrary, we have been inundated with hordes of preachers declaring peace, prosperity, and blessings upon the people of God. We have flocked to their seminars, bought their books and videos, and paid them money to hear more. For a season, it seemed so prophetic -- we have found a new path into God's prosperity that all the old-timers from the brush arbor revival days were never aware of.

They preached the Fear of the Lord and a crucified walk of sacrifice, but we have heaped up to us teachers that have illuminated a new, better way of "love" that is so much more enlightening.

But now, like Gideon, we wonder where are all the miracles that we used to see? Where are the piles of discarded crutches, the packed altars with broken hearts, the supernatural outpourings on our services and all-night prayer meetings? For that matter, where are our prayer meetings? We are in the midst of the drought, and we are just now noticing our dry throats and cracked lips that once were anointed with the Spirit of God.

After three and a half years of drought when there was no moving of the Spirit of God in Israel, Elijah called forth a final showdown with Baal.

Judgment was set upon a mountaintop where the fire of God fell and devoured the priests and prophets of the established churches of the land.

And still, there was no revival – just a mumbled acknowledgment of what was obvious but no heartfelt repentance. After all, not only had the people just witnessed the death of their beloved local pastors and prophets but, with them, the demise of their hopes for prosperity and a life of religious ease.

But then Elijah turns to Ahab and tells him that he hears the sound of an abundance of rain.

I heard that sound last night.

It was the sound of desperate hearts crying out to God to please forgive us for our idolatry, to have mercy on us and send a revival, not just for us, but for all those souls out there who have been lost because of our apostate ways. I could hear Nehemiah and Daniel's echoes when they too, had cried out in repentance for God to have mercy on His people and restore us again.

There was a melding of voices as I could feel them funneling straight up to the Throne of God, driven by the sorrow of tears that flowed from broken hearts. And then, intermingled with them, was the drip, drip, drip of the tears of God falling to the Earth for His people.

It was the sound of an abundance of rain.

No Burger King Salvation

But ye are not in the flesh, but in the Spirit, if so be that the Spirit of God dwell in you. Now if any man have not the Spirit of Christ, he is none of His. Romans 8:9

"Well, how about doing good works, like giving canned goods and clothes to the poor?" "Nope. You have to have the Spirit of God in you."

"How about going to church every week?" "Sorry, you have to be in the Spirit of God, not the spirit of your church."

"But I believe in God, so I will go to Heaven." "The devils in Hell also believe, and at least they tremble. It doesn't do them any good, does it?"

"Yeah, but I'm not a devil. I am actually a regular good guy. I don't smoke or chew. I don't drink or commit adultery. I don't cheat on my taxes ... I'm just a normal, decent human being." "Well, good luck. You're gonna need it because all that still won't punch your ticket into Heaven."

"What about all the Christian books that I read? Isn't that good?" " I don't know if that's good or not, but it doesn't make you a Christian and it can't save your soul."

"Yes, but I have a fish on my bumper, I wear a Christian T-Shirt on Saturday, and I go to all the

Christian music concerts. I'm even a Promise Keeper. Doesn't that count?" "It might count with them, but as God tells us in Malachi 3:16, He only counts those who fear the Lord and keep His commandments."

- "Yes, but I'm a Bible scholar, and I know all kinds of deep, hidden scriptural truths. Surely that makes me right with God."

    "No, only the Blood of Jesus Christ can make you right with God. The rest of that theological stuff only serves to make you accountable. Nice try, though."

- "What about all my good works?"

    "What about them? Are you trying to equate your good works with what Jesus did on the Cross?"

- "Well, I know I'm right because I hold to the correct doctrine and do all the things that I'm supposed to do right down to all the Levitical ordinances."

    "That's what the Pharisees said, and they're burning in Hell right now."

- "But if I say all the right things, and believe all the right things, and do all the right things, then what's the problem?"

    "The problem is that there is no power in anything you can do or say that can save your soul. The only thing that has the power to do that is the Blood of Jesus Christ, and to avail yourself of that you have to surrender, repent and allow yourself to be broken at the foot of that Cross, and accept His salvation by asking Jesus Christ to forgive you and wash away your sins in His blood."

You must, absolutely must, be born-again. That is when the Spirit of God can enter into your heart and be inside you. It is written that only those who are led by the Spirit can call themselves the sons of God (Rom. 8:14)

You can't have it your way.

"For the Kingdom of God is not in word, but in power." 1Corinthians 4:20

Jerusalem

> *Now the children of Judah had fought against Jerusalem, and had taken it, and smitten it with the edge of the sword, and set the city on fire. Judges 1:8*

Whenever Jerusalem comes up in Scripture, I always pay attention. This is Zion, the habitation of God; it is where God chose to place His name. Jerusalem is special.

Jerusalem is on Mount Moriah, the place where Abraham was called to sacrifice his son, Isaac, but thanks to the mercy and the eternal plan of God, Abraham was able to look up and "see the place afar off." When he did, he turned to his men and told them that he and the lad would return. I have always believed that Abraham looked afar off, not in distance, but in time. He saw Calvary.

Jerusalem is the place where God established a covenant between Himself and mankind when His Son became the sacrifice and "passed between the parts" in the Biblical tradition of a covenant as He hung between the thieves and paid the price of blood.

Yes, Jerusalem has always been special; and will continue to be so.

Originally, Jerusalem was given to the tribe of Benjamin for their inheritance, but they lost it soon after taking it. What bothers me is that they let it go so easily. It is written in Judges 1:21 that Benjamin couldn't regain the city, and it remained in the hands of the uncircumcised until David conquered it and established it as the centerpiece of Zion. It was taken from Benjamin and given to Judah.

How could they let that happen? Perhaps they never realized how important the place of Jerusalem was to God to let it slip through their fingers. I guess it just wasn't that big of a deal to them.

Is it any different today?

Once upon a time, we had a grip on the Spirit that was the centerpiece for the Zion of today. But we let it slip out of our fingers. We have left off to fear the Lord, have become too polite to preach about Hell, and we've become so sophisticated and nice to each other that we are afraid to call for the people of God to come to a place of repentance. We won't even acknowledge our sin. Lukewarm mediocrity is dragging us to Hell.

As a result, there is no outpouring of the Holy Spirit from on High; we just have "church as usual." There is no supernatural healing power of God in our churches, only gradual medical treatments from medical professionals.

There are no altars packed with lost souls crying out to God with all their hearts for Salvation. Instead, we have "pity" lines in their place for people to complain about the same problems that they did not have the spiritual strength to overcome the week before. And then have the gall to ask for blessings. Have they forgotten that the Altar of God is not a place of singing and dancing but a place of sacrifice, blood, and death?

There are no prayer meetings anymore where the people of God would gather together to cry out to the Lord and shake the foundations of the Throne of God for revival, for lost souls, for a great and mighty move of God. No, we have replaced them with Christian entertainers, self-help motivational speakers, and other Gypsies of such like.

True, not everyone is backslidden. On Sunday, I went to a little church in a small town in Texas and heard about the fear of the Lord, the power of the Blood of Jesus Christ, repentance for sin, a call for a prayer meeting that evening, and wonder of wonders, an Altar Call for the lost! And, praise the Lord, I felt the Spirit of the Lord move in services! What God can do with a little church that has the boldness to declare the truth! He can take a little shepherd that is simple enough to have true faith and zeal, and He can make him a king.

As for the rest of us, we lost Jerusalem somewhere in the process, ... and I'm not sure that we even care.

Surely, Zion will be recovered, and a revival will come, but when it does, that place of Zion will be taken away from you and given to those whom God raises up in your place.

Excuse

There have been a few questions that I have continued to wonder about over the years. One is why some people get saved, and others do not. And then I wonder why some people, after they have been saved, don't stay saved!

The Lord answered that one for me when I was very young in the Lord, "Some people care, and some people don't. It's as simple as that." I was stunned when I received that answer from God – it was simple, direct, and profound. And, really, that's just the way it is.

Still, you have to wonder why.

I've witnessed my heart out to many people over the years, but not everybody wants to get saved. I don't get it. To me, the choice is such a simple one to make:

#1, If you believe in God, then believe what He says. To refuse means that you are going to wind up in Hell.

#2, If you don't believe in God, there's a simple test to see if He is really there – just get saved, and you'll feel the Spirit of God save your soul. Then you'll know – you'll really know!

Sounds simple to me. Maybe it's not God they don't believe. Maybe it's me. Okay, but I'm not telling anyone something that is new or strange. People have been getting saved for centuries. We can't all be crazy! Isn't it worth putting it to the test to find out if it is really the truth? After all, if it is and you refuse it, you will burn in Hell. If not, what have you got to lose?

But some people just don't care.

Then you have others who have actually gone down to the altar and have tasted of the Spirit of God but, after a while, decide to abandon it. What happened? Did they get distracted by other things and forget about Eternity? Or did they think that all they had to do was say a prayer once in their life, and that was it?

I have found that people will follow their hearts, and if their hearts do not hunger for righteousness and Truth, they will follow something else. People are going to believe what they want to believe in spite of the facts, and they will use the Bible to justify it. I don't think there is any better definition of stupidity than that, but that's human nature for you.

I have another question: just exactly where does God draw the line between those who are going to Heaven and those who will go to Hell? There is a dividing line somewhere that separates the sheep from the goats, and I want to make sure I am on the right side of that line. Obviously, just knowing <u>about</u> the Truth is not what gets you to Heaven – you must walk the walk. The path is clearly written in the Word of God, but how few are willing to take it to heart.

Maybe it all comes back around to what the Lord showed me in the very beginning: some people care, and some people do not. It's as simple as that. Not everyone is going to Heaven. You have to be hungry for truth.

I guess that is how God tests your heart. If you're hungry, you will seek the face of God; if you're not, you'll find some excuse to pursue other things.

And an excuse, after all, is simply saying you don't care.

"As the hart panteth after the water brooks, so panteth my soul after thee, O God." Psalm 42:1

Sodomites

> *"And he broke down the houses of the sodomites, that were by the house of the LORD, where the women wove hangings for the grove."* 2 Kings 23:7

Imagine that! The homosexuals were setting up shop right by the House of God, just like they are today. I guess the more things change, the more they stay the same.

Today, however, if you dare say anything against them, you are guilty of "homophobia", and you are also a bigoted, narrow-minded hatemonger who does not understand the meaning of Love. Don't you know that Jesus preached Love?

I gotta tell you, I got homophobia real bad. Yep, scared to death. And I'm all the rest of those ugly things they accuse me of too. Plus, I'm a bunch of other stuff they haven't mentioned yet. I'm their worst nightmare.

There is a satanic agenda that is pushing this perverse demon possession into our schools, our TV and movies, our government, and good grief, even the Boy Scouts. I see it applauded by the liberal left as being an enlightened state of mind that there is absolutely nothing wrong with. We are eating this stuff for breakfast, lunch, and dinner!

Yeah, I'm scared because, although I can understand why these reprobates really believe this stuff, what worries me is why Christians don't have enough guts to call these devils as what they really are. We have been sold this bill of goods that we aren't supposed to offend anyone, so we politely let them roll right over us and take over a society that was once founded on the Gospel of Jesus Christ.

Guess who convinced us that Christians are supposed to be nice and not offend anyone. Let me give you a clue: it wasn't God. As for me, I'm not a nice guy – I'm not interested in being nice, and I'm not trying to be nice. I just believe in calling a spade a spade, and if I hit a nerve in the process, then that's just too bad.

Oh, but didn't you know that they were Christians too? Oh really? Is that why God said they were worthy of death? Gosh, poor ol' God. He must be homophobic too.

Old King Josiah had the right idea – clear 'em out of the church and run them out of town! Well, we can't do that today because we got the ACLU to dictate our morals for us.

We are living in a time where the issues between light and darkness, good and evil, holy and profane, are polarizing in intensity. The middle ground is constantly pulled toward one or the other side. To sit on the sidelines like some quiet little church mouse plays right into Satan's plans.

Jude 1:3 says we must earnestly contend for the truth, and Jesus said that if you weren't with Him, you were against Him (Matt. 12:30). That still applies. If you are silent in these times of controversy, you will hear the cries of those you could have saved as they descend into Hell. And you might end up being right behind them.

There's a shifting in the wind, the battle is picking up, and the lines are forming on the battlefield. We are entering into a new dispensation of time, and we are choosing which side we will be on right now. Either you hate evil, or you make excuses for it.

> *"Woe unto them that call evil good, and good evil; that put darkness for light, and light for darkness; that put bitter for sweet, and sweet for bitter!"*
> *Isaiah 5:20*

Charley

Charley died yesterday on Mother's Day on his way to church.

Why does stuff like this happen? We want to believe that our universe is organized and fair; that when you do good, good things happen, and that if not, then you reap what you sow. We want to believe that God is in charge of human events (at least ours, anyway) and that everything will turn out like the fairy tales that our mothers read to us when we were kids. But that is just not the way Life goes.

Charley was two weeks from graduating High School, engaged to be married, and had what seemed to be a bright future ahead of him. A tall, lanky, quiet kid, he never created any waves and was the kind of kid that you would be glad to be part of your neighborhood. Just a regular guy. This was not something that you would have ever expected to happen ... but then, you never do.

But there was one good thing about all this – Charley had just gotten saved. He was baptized just two weeks ago and was filled with the excitement of a newly saved Christian. He had just started attending an exciting new church in Maypearl that the Spirit of the Lord was moving in. It was so wonderful to him that he had actually found a place where you could actually feel the presence of the Holy Ghost, and so he had given his life to Jesus Christ. Now all he wanted to do was serve the Lord.

Now, I don't want to say that this was perfect timing or anything crass like that, but if this had happened a few weeks ago, the results would have been quite different. But God knew. And now, Charley is in a place where nothing on this Earth can ever compare to the glories that he is walking in the midst of. Given the chance, I doubt that he would want to come back.

Was this just a senseless anomaly? Is there any good that could come out of what seems to be such a waste? Was God paying attention to something else at the time and let this thing slip by Him?

Oh, I don't think so. For one thing, I would bet that <u>Charley</u> doesn't care right now. There might be grief here amongst his friends and family, but there is rejoicing in Heaven. He didn't have his life cut short – he had it glorified. He didn't lose the bright future he had here before him – he entered into it.

As for those who knew him, he has left a testimony that will not be easily forgotten, one that the Lord can use to deal with other souls who have not been saved, that there is a point in Life that we will all come to when we will stand before God and give account for our sins, and it can happen at any time.

Death is not a scheduled event for any of us, nor have we signed a lease on life that we will have any certain amount of days to live. The only thing that we can be sure of is today. Betting on tomorrow is worse than gambling away your eyeballs on the throw of a dice, for once you have crossed over into Eternity, there is no coming back to do it over again. People are lying on morgue slabs right now with shopping lists in their pockets but never made it home with the groceries.

There are no regrets with God and no future without Him. Just ask Charley. He gave the best witness in the world for Jesus Christ – Charley was ready, and he died in the arms of His Savior.

"Precious in the sight of the LORD is the death of his saints." Psalms 116:15

Draw Me

> *"Draw me, we will run after thee: the king hath brought me into his chambers: we will be glad and rejoice in thee, we will remember thy love more than wine: the upright love thee."* Song of Solomon 1:4

What was the real difference between David and Saul? What did the disciples have that the Pharisees could never grasp? Why is it that some churches are alive with the Spirit of God while others only have religion? What is the difference between those who claim to believe God and those who are filled with His Spirit?

It has to do with how they define the love of God.

Anyone can say they love God, raise their hands, and sway back and forth to the Praise & Worship songs, but that does not constitute the real love of God -- that is an emotional display.

Proclaiming zeal for God isn't the principle thing either. Saul claimed to be zealous for God but was drowned out by the bleating of sheep. Instead of complete obedience to God's command to slay all that the enemy possessed, his focus remained centered on himself. David, on the other hand, worshipped God.

Religious knowledge doesn't constitute the love of God, either. The Pharisees had devoted their entire existence to the study of the Torah and built layers of rules to keep themselves from crossing any scriptural lines, but the Bible says that their mistake was in that they tried to establish their own righteousness rather than submitting to the righteousness of God (Rom. 10:3).

The disciples of Jesus were not so self-possessed, not so sophisticated in their carnal religiousness, and not so intent on the fruit that is desired to make one wise -- they just loved Jesus Christ.

Throughout time, you can see the difference between those who seek to be religious and those who seek for that secret place of the Most High God. Each claims to love God but has very different approaches. With one, it is all about themselves, while with the other, it is all about God.

The true love of God does not lie in carnal adherence to tenets of doctrine or traditions, in pursuit of knowledge or power, in the segregation of denominational thinking, or even in gushing displays of emotional affection. The essence of the love of God lies in surrender.

To surrender means to give up your ways, your ideas, and your perception of life and religion. You have to love God so much that you choose to give up

-- completely give up -- and empty all the "you" out of you so it can be completely filled with Him, and render yourself invisible so that the glory of God can shine out of you. You choose to die for Him, just as He died for you. You love God that much.

Dive into the Spirit of God, and let God lead you into all righteousness and true wisdom instead of trying to figure it out for yourself. Let His Spirit overwhelm you and cover you with His feathers. Surrender. Your reward is not in what you can be in Him, but what He can be in you.

When you do that, the glory of God will fill your soul and will fill your church. You will not be seen as a church where people meet but as a place where the Spirit of God blazes with His Glory. It will be a place where you can feel the glow on those who have been drawn by Him, and Him alone, and have run after God to be brought into His secret chambers.

Surrender. That is the place where you fall into the love of God with great abandon.

Guesswork

> *"And the LORD said unto Moses, Go, get thee down; for thy people, which thou broughtest out of the land of Egypt, have corrupted themselves: They have turned aside quickly out of the way which I commanded them: they have made them a molten calf, and have worshipped it, and have sacrificed thereunto, and said, These be thy gods, O Israel, which have brought thee up out of the land of Egypt."* Exodus 32:7,8

As a kid growing up, I went through several denominational churches and believed everything I was told, as children will believe what they are told when it comes from a credible source such as their parents or their Pastor. But there came a time when I began to wonder where the proof was.

If God was so big, powerful, and omnipresent, then why didn't He show Himself so we could all know for sure? Not ever getting a good answer, I dropped my belief in God.

What really puzzled me was why so many people who did believe in God still hung on to their beliefs so tenaciously even though they could never prove it. They would tell me that it wasn't something you could put to the test. Then why believe it?

Faith is a strange thing to someone who doesn't have it.

The human sciences of Psychology and Sociology are rife with seemingly intelligent guesses to explain why people hang on so dearly to religion. Since I could find no solid evidence to contradict them, I fell into their hypnotic sway. It seemed there really was no God, and people of Faith were only hanging on to an unsustainable hope for some psychological reason.

It sounded good then, and it still convinces people today. What a pity to hang your hopes for Life on something that was merely ethereal.

Yes, but how much more of a pity is it to lose all hope itself.

Religion, therefore, seemed to me like a good diversion to answer the unanswerable questions and settle the nagging questions in your soul. Nothing more; nothing less.

But then I got saved, and everything changed!

I discovered that Salvation is not just a statement of belief, but it is a supernatural experience with God that changes your whole life. When it happens to you, there is no explaining it – it just happens. Then, as you pursue God, His presence becomes more and more real, and life in the Spirit of God is no longer a matter of guesswork – it becomes a reality.

Then why are so many churches so dead? You would think that when people heard of a church where the Spirit of God is flowing so strong, they would flock there. Maybe it's easier to settle into a complacent faith that does not challenge you. You see, once you get a taste of the real thing and realize that God is really there, then the realization sets in that you're going to have to change your ways.

Ahhh, now it begins to make sense. If we want to hang onto our sins, our complacency, and our ego, then we will have to come up with some way to justify our lifestyle. We need to find a religion that will allow us to tie up those old nagging questions without compelling us to change. We find a church that will allow us to believe what we want to believe, and then we settle into it.

People love religion because it is so easy. If all we had to do was count a few beads, show up once a week, and make an outward show, we could then call ourselves Christians and be satisfied. On the other hand, if we really want to feel spiritual, we can get deep into some vain genealogies and intricacies of doctrine to bolster our egos. Neither way gives Life.

There are those, however, who are not satisfied with "church as usual" but want something real. They are the ones who will seek for a tangible relationship with God, and when they find it, they will not let go. It becomes the essence of Life to them and the answer to all those nagging questions that God has planted in our hearts.

What a wonderful thing it is to feel the Spirit of God flow over you and through you! It is like plunging into the Fountain of Life. All questions are dissolved. God is real!

Transcending all religious dogma and doctrine, only the Spirit of God gives Life. One thing I've noticed about those who are wrapped up in concocted theologies, no matter how much they quote the Bible, it seems they never talk about their experience with the Spirit of God. They can't feel it because they don't have it.

On the other hand, when you run into someone who knows what it is like to have the tangible Spirit of God in their life, they can't stop talking about it. Hmmm, I wonder which one has God and which one just has religion. And guess which one counts on the Day of Judgment.

We are coming out of a very long and dry period in the churches where there has been very little moving of the Holy Ghost, but that is beginning to change. The Lord is beginning to raise up some places where He is answering the cry of those who have been hungry for so long, and He is moving in wonderful supernatural ways.

Those who refuse to surrender their pride and their long-established traditions will say that it is nothing but emotionalism. They will resist the move of God so they can hang on to their dead traditions and not have to change their ways. That's the way it has always been in the past, and I'm sure it will be the same today. How sad that so many would choose to eat off the Tree of Knowledge of Good and Evil rather than the Tree of Life.

But for those of you who are hungry for the real thing, I say choose Life. The Word of God is the only Truth there is. That's enough for me.

Reading

> *Behold, the days come, saith the Lord GOD, that I will send a famine in the land, not a famine of bread, nor a thirst for water, but of hearing the words of the LORD: And they shall wander from sea to sea, and from the north even to the east, they shall run to and fro to seek the word of the LORD, and shall not find it. Amos 8:11,12*

One of the greatest challenges I see facing the life of Christianity is the lack of reading the Word of God.

Now, how could that be, seeing that there are churches everywhere and Bibles are found in almost every home? Does this really apply to us since so many profess that they believe in Jesus Christ?

Let's face it, the scripture above is a severe prophecy and not one to be taken lightly. The haunting aspect of this prophecy is that it lies like a dark cloud over the entire world – including us.

I am amazed at the lack of Biblical depth I have found amongst Christians. Many deacons and associate pastors have little more than a surface knowledge of the Bible and rely more upon what they read in other books and what they think rather than what is written in the Word of God. Why?

Because they do not read it as if their life depended on it!

The Bible is not a textbook; it is a source of Life. It is not merely a guide to successful living; it is a Light so that we can see things as they really are. Neither is it a book to answer questions; rather, it is a book that raises questions to probe the answers of Life.

When you are filled with it, the Word of God does something inside you that lifts the curtain of this world so that you can think, see, and feel from the perspective of Eternity. When you fill yourself with it, you ingest the very nature of God and you are changed from the inside out. Conversely, when you do not read it, you are left to your own perceptions of what you think the Truth should be.

To attempt to pray without the power that comes from reading the Word of God is an effort that is anemic and shallow. To sing and dance before the Lord without being filled with the Word of God is little more than a show of superficiality. Is it a small wonder that we find ourselves more entertained with modern Christian music that carries a nice tune and has rejected the old-fashioned Blood-washed Gospel songs? We no longer feel the power in those worship songs because we are not filled with the same Spirit that wrote them. And that comes from devouring the Word.

The Word of God gives you power to pray past your flesh; it gives you power to rip off the garments of religion to walk in His Spirit; it gives you wisdom and discernment to see through false doctrines, and it creates a desire deep in your heart to seek the face of God.

Snacking on the Word of God only serves to make you accountable, but to devour it as the source of Life gives you power. That is why Satan has sold us a bill of goods that we can get by simply knowing the basics without ever diving into the depths of the Word to feel the change that it makes in your heart.

In Cana of Galilee, Jesus commanded the waterpots to be filled up to the brim – all the way to overflowing – before the water could be turned into wine. We are those waterpots of stone and the water is the Word of God. 99% is not enough. You have to be filled to experience the miracle that can happen in your life.

But so many of us are satisfied with convenience instead of overcoming our fleshly excuses. As a result, we find the Bible everywhere, but there is a famine for hearing what it really says.

Fruit of Righteousness

"The fruit of the righteous is a tree of life; and he that winneth souls is wise." Proverbs 11:30

Over the years, I have developed a habit of reading the chapter in Proverbs that corresponds to today's date. There are 31 chapters, and generally 31 days to a month.

There always seems to be something in that day's chapter that I will need that day. I don't know how that works, but it seems to happen more often than not, so each morning, I look forward to seeing what the message will be for today.

This morning, I noticed the proverb that stated that the fruit of righteousness is a tree. Huh? The fruit is a tree? That caught my attention.

Not only that, but it is the same tree that we find in the Garden of Eden.

Now, I have spent a lot of time preaching about the difference between the Tree of Knowledge and the Tree of Life. While one is a tree desired to make one wise, the other requires us to let go of our own wisdom and understanding and turn ourselves completely over to God.

Isn't it interesting that the second part of the proverb tells us that real wisdom is not to be found in how much stuff we know but in the winning of souls? That is a vast difference in perspective.

You cannot win souls with carnal knowledge, theological degrees, conspiracy theories, mental gymnastics of numerologies, or stiff adherence to old traditions. You have to be in the Spirit of God to be able to deal with human souls, for only the Spirit of God can reach deep into their hearts and draw them to the Cross.

Intelligent appeals that address mental reasoning may convince many that the Bible is really the Truth, but unless that is accompanied with Holy Ghost conviction, you won't see any broken hearts at the altar. It is the power of the Blood of Jesus Christ that saves souls – nothing else – and that is only manifested through the "foolishness" of preaching the cross.

While it may be fascinating to hear yourself spout off theological nonsense and learn "new things," you have to be in the Spirit of God to bring Life to a lost soul, and that requires a broken, crucified walk that denies the flesh and yields only to the Spirit of God.

Since the Tree of Life is found in the fruit of the righteous, not the fruit of religion and theology, then if I want to eat off the Tree of Life, I have to walk in righteousness. So how do I do that? Is it simply a matter of "just believe in Jesus," and everything will just miraculously be alright? What does the Lord require?

The Bible says that it is through the fear of the Lord that men depart from evil (Prov. 16:6) and that the fear of God is wisdom (Job 28:28). That's the key that unlocks the door to a real, inspired walk in the Spirit – the fear of Almighty God!

You know, it strikes me that if our preachers would emphasize the fear of God, we might find that our altars would attract lost souls.

But then, they are educated men, so perhaps they are just too sophisticated to give in to that old-fashioned message of the real fear of the Lord.

Which may be why their sermons are dry, their churches are sterile, and their altars are empty.

James, Peter, & John

"And he suffered no man to follow him, save Peter, and James, and John the brother of James." Mark 5:37

Although Jesus had hundreds of followers and disciples, he only picked twelve to be the ones who would establish the foundations of His church. Of the twelve, Peter, James and John were the inside circle.

I never gave much thought to it other than I just figured that these guys were just pretty lucky. They got to go with Jesus into some pretty special places.

They were the ones who were at the mount of Transfiguration and saw Jesus as He really is, the anointed Son of God, standing there with Moses and Elijah. How amazing that was! But they were also there in the depth of His passion in Gethsemane. They saw it all.

I often wondered how they got along with each other. Did you ever notice how different their personalities were? I can just imagine Peter being turned off with John because he was too sweet and syrupy, while James was probably exasperated with Peter's rashness. And John probably waltzed right past the quirks of both James and Peter without even paying attention. Who knows? I suppose we'll hear some hilarious stories when we get to Heaven ... that is if you're going there.

It struck me the other day, however, that these three represent the basic personality types that all of us fit into to one extent or another. A quick read through the New Testament and you can see how their differences apply to us all. Perhaps that is why Jesus chose them.

James was the organizer of the bunch. If there was anyone that could be construed as legalistic, James was the guy. He is, after all, the one who wrote about faith without works and that if you offend in one point, you are guilty of all. I get the feeling that James liked everything in order. He probably would've made a great lawyer. That is probably why he was chosen as the first head of the church at Jerusalem.

Peter, on the other hand, was strong in spirit, often choleric in nature, and often fueled by the fiery nature of his own passion. I have often had the feeling that his zeal drove him past caring what anyone else thought. He was the kind of guy that just told it like it was and let the chips fall where they may, just like in 2nd Peter when he was pulling no punches in exposing heretics. He had his failures, but his drive and energy always drove him back into the fight.

John, of course, is always a picture of someone who had a soft heart, not only toward Jesus but toward everyone. Although it is easy to see that he had a much softer approach, he did draw a strong line between right and wrong. Famous for the scripture, "God is Love," John went on to explain that the Love of God meant keeping God's commandments, and if someone didn't do that, ... well, you weren't even supposed to shake his hand.

I look over the Christians I've known, and I see all three personalities manifested. While we may lean toward those who are most like ourselves, let us not assume that one type is any better than another. While I may be suited to a more hard-nosed approach like Peter, I need to understand that there are many people like John who see things differently. There may be those like James who get exasperated at my wild and flighty ways but who thank God for my passion. And Dear God, thank you for the James in our midst! Somebody has to keep things organized!

Let us all remember that God created us with all the wonderful differences that we have so that we may rejoice in each other's strengths and come together as the Body of Christ.

James, Peter, and John were as different as three guys can be, but they established a foundation that has lasted for 2,000 years.

Dross

> *"Take away the dross from the silver, and there shall come forth a vessel for the finer."* Proverbs 25:4

I suppose we all have areas in our lives that we wish we could gain some victory over. I know I have mine. I constantly struggle with the gap between what I am and what I want to be.

I have always believed in the power of reading God's Word to the fullest and the emersion of deep prevailing prayer. I figure that only the Spirit of God can bring us to that place that we really aspire to, certainly not the puny efforts of our own flesh.

Oh, how I wish I could squeeze myself into that discipline of spending hours a day seeking the face of the Lord. Unfortunately, I fail just about every day, but thank God, at least He keeps that carrot out in front of my face to keep me running after it. That makes for a miserable excuse, I know, but at least I have never quit trying.

I have noticed in our modern Christianity, however, that we have been slowly led to believe that somehow, we can attain to a place of power in God without the effort.

Let me explain. I have long decried the shift in our focus to a more loving, kinder, gentler God than what our forefathers preached about. God is no longer the great Almighty God who is to be feared but has now become our "Daddy" who wants to smother us with His unconditional Love.

Maybe I've missed something here, and perhaps my detractors are right. It seems that God has changed His attitude and is no longer the God of judgment we've read about in so many passages. Who knows? Maybe He figured that the old way just wasn't working anymore, and we needed a different approach to draw us to Him. Or maybe things have changed, and our society is hurting so much that we need more love and less judgment. Perhaps there is some truth to that.

But I am still stuck on the scriptures that exhort us to overcome, as it repeatedly says in Revelations. Perhaps I have leaned too much on discipline and not enough on mercy, but I just can't abandon the one so I can give myself over to the other. I believe there are billows of mercy with God, but there is also a price for everything you want from Him. Mercy must be mixed with a contrite heart and a broken spirit for it to bear forth the fruits of the Spirit of God.

One place I have seen this new "easy" attitude manifested is in our altar calls. So many times, I hear the preacher call those of us forward who "want more in God," and many people that are genuinely hungry for more of God come forward to be prayed over. I have felt the Spirit of God move dramatically during these calls, and I believe wholeheartedly in them – but is that all there is? Do we then go home secure in the belief that we have just been elevated to a higher place in our faith? Is it that easy?

I don't think so. The dross has to be taken away before you can shine as pure silver, and that can only be done by going through the fire – something a bit more substantial than just a quick, one-shot altar call. The Blood of Jesus Christ paid for our salvation and opened the door for us to walk in victory, but it is up to us to take up the Cross and go on from there.

Offering our congregation a light and easy solution to the desperate cries of their hearts is like Proverbs 25:20 **"As he that taketh away a garment in cold weather, … so is he that singeth songs to an heavy heart."**

Take away the garments of righteousness by not calling for repentance, and all you are doing is singing songs to a heavy heart that is crying out to get right with God. Is it a small wonder that we have an anemic Church that lacks the power to claim victory and overcome our weaknesses?

There is no instant, cheap solution to walking in the overcoming power of God. You get what you pay for.

Feeding our people with anything less than that is like feeding a hungry soul with food that has no substance – it may taste good, but it will never give you strength and will never satiate that gnawing hunger in your soul.

Ireland

> *"It's better to polarize some shoppers than to generate mass apathy."*
> *(Chris Denove, commenting on a survey about the habits of retail shoppers.)*

A friend of mine sent me this tidbit with the comment that perhaps we should apply this to training our preachers. I had to laugh. They could sure use it, but somehow, I fear that it would never catch on. Preachers are generally too afraid of offending their congregations, much like Adam, who listened to his wife instead of taking a strong stand.

The results, however, are not quite as humorous.

Another friend of mine, Jack McGee, a courageous minister in Northern Ireland, has been face-to-face with the bloody effects of a religious confrontation that has gone far beyond the religious arena where it started.

Civil war broke out in Northern Ireland in the name of God, clothed with political purposes but fueled by conflicting churches. It is now bringing forth the fruits of sectarian murder that is swiftly overcoming any effect that the churches have control over anymore. Several more people have been murdered in the last few days, even after the so-called truce by the IRA.

What happened to the strong ministers of the Gospel that should have had a controlling influence on this continuing bloodshed? In seeking political compromises for a solution, they have lost their reliance on the one thing that can change the hardened hearts of a desperate society – the power of a Gospel that is delivered in the strength and boldness of men and women who fear God.

If you simply tell Satan to play nice, he will laugh in your face. He will return your polite manners by cranking up the fires of hatred even more. War finds no place for nice guys.

Jack is different. He has stood in the midst of the conflict and has upheld the Blood-Stained Banner of Jesus Christ as the only solution to counteract the long-term effects of religions that have been weakened by a lack of holy boldness.

When we relegate the Fear of God to a sideline doctrine, we lose our courage and our holy boldness to fight for the righteousness of God. Satan sees the weakened walls of our defenses and easily knocks them down.

Once he has taken possession of a battleground, it is not so easy to regain it. Singing songs that you will stamp on the devil and take back what he has stolen may make you feel good but has little effect in the real world. It takes courageous men and women of conviction who are willing to stand up in the power of the Holy Ghost and fight.

Such warriors are not forged in Bible Colleges or in the sedate confines of religious complacency. They are forged in fire, warfare, and conflict. They are warhorses in God who rise to the challenge when they smell the smoke of battle.

I believe that it is better to be in the thick of fierce battle and pay the price of war than to sit on the bleachers of detached apostasy and cheer your warriors on. Victories are not won on the sidelines.

Hast thou given the horse strength? Hast thou clothed his neck with thunder? Canst thou make him afraid as a grasshopper?

The glory of his nostrils is terrible. He paweth in the valley, and rejoiceth in his strength: he goeth on to meet the armed men. He mocketh at fear, and is not affrighted; neither turneth he back from the sword.

The quiver rattleth against him, the glittering spear and the shield. He swalloweth the ground with fierceness and rage: neither believeth he that it is the sound of the trumpet.

He saith among the trumpets, Ha, ha; and he smelleth the battle afar off, the thunder of the captains, and the shouting. Job 39:19-25

May God raise up warriors in your midst like unto you, Jack, to raise the Stained Blood Banner and carry the battle to the enemy to claim victory with the fierceness of those who fight with the holy boldness that only comes from the Throne of God.

Chiropractor's Daughter

"Daddy, why doesn't God answer our prayers as soon as we pray them?"

Boy, that's a good one for you! An old chiropractor in Texas told me about this question that his daughter had asked him.

I sometimes wonder if God didn't create children just to keep us humble.

As adults, we sometimes tend to bypass hard questions and accept them as the vague things of life when we can't answer them. Children, however, are more direct in their views of life and haven't yet learned that there are some things that you have to just accept.

I am reminded of the story of Fred Smith, the founder of Federal Express. This is the guy who received a C on his college term paper that outlined the idea of an overnight delivery service and was told by his professor that it just wouldn't work. Fred just did it anyway. He never accepted the fact that there are some things in life you must settle for.

In the last 70 or 80 years, we have kept up the appearances of church, secure in the knowledge that the Word of God is true and God is really there. We go to church and follow the paths that were laid out before us by our forefathers, but the results just are not the same. Still, we show up every week because that is what we have accepted as being the thing that we are supposed to do to be a Christian.

Increasingly, however, there is a generation that is rising up that wants to know why we don't have the same experiences that we have heard were so commonplace, not only in the Book of Acts, but even amongst our church forefathers. Where is the outpouring of the Holy Ghost that we have heard so much about? Where are the piles of crutches that once were discarded outside the tent revivals? What happened to all the miracles that we are told used to happen all the time? And where, oh where, are the altar calls that were packed with repentant sinners?

How do we answer our youth when they point to the Bible and hold up the unanswered promises of God to us? When they remind us of the miraculous times that forged our denominations in the fires of revival, how do we explain our current dearth?

This generation is increasingly dissatisfied with our answers. They are not willing to simply accept things as they are. They want to know the why! If it is written in the Word of God, if the promises of God are written into Eternity, then where is the miraculous presence of God? Theological dissertations, cheap religious excuses, and sedate educated answers from learned men who hold Ph.D.'s (read that as "Piled Higher and Deeper") will not do. They are not willing to accept unbelief as a doctrine of faith.

Where did God go? Why are our churches content with the liturgical requiems they pass off for services? If the presence of the Holy Ghost was a tangible vibrancy in times past, then why can't we have it today?

It is not that God has left us; we have left God. We created our own golden calves called denominational religion and left Moses on the mountain with God. Our organizational abilities have taken us on a path that has led away from the raw, childlike faith that relied on nothing but God, and as a result, has led us to the flat, sparse landscape of a spiritual desert.

That old Texas chiropractor said he stepped back for a moment and prayed and then turned to his daughter and replied, "If God answered our prayers right away, honey, we wouldn't realize how much we need Him."

How true. God is waiting for a people that need Him. Revival will come only to those with childlike faith who refuse to accept the way things are but will storm the heavenlies to force God into a corner and demand an outpouring of the Holy Ghost.

When we realize how much we need Him, we will get our answer.

And the angel of the LORD appeared unto him, and said unto him, The LORD is with thee, thou mighty man of valor.

And Gideon said unto him, Oh my Lord, if the LORD be with us, why then is all this befallen us? and where be all his miracles which our fathers told us of, saying, Did not the LORD bring us up from Egypt? but now the LORD hath forsaken us, and delivered us into the hands of the Midianites.

And the LORD looked upon him, and said, Go in this thy might, and thou shalt save Israel from the hand of the Midianites: have not I sent thee?

(Judges 6:12-14)

Plumbline is set

> *"And the LORD said unto me, Amos, what seest thou? And I said, A plumbline. Then said the Lord, Behold, I will set a plumbline in the midst of my people Israel: I will not again pass by them any more:"* Amos 7:8

It's scary business when the Lord tells you that He has had enough. That's it. Finished. Done.

The longsuffering of the Lord is incredible in its depth and duration … but there is a limit. When we stretch God's mercy to the breaking point, two things happen: God becomes more and more frustrated, while we become more convinced that everything will continue the way it has, and we can pursue our own ways.

Consider how much mercy God had on the Israelites. Not only were they delivered from Egypt with a mighty hand, but God personally gave them His laws and statutes, which would give them life and blessings. When they rebelled, He sent judges and prophets and deliverers to call them back to Him. Even His judgments were acts of mercy.

But their repentance was always temporary. They would quickly go back to their old fleshly ways, dismiss their judges, and kill their prophets so they could go back to their old sins. Always, however, they kept an outside show of religion – they just mollified it to excuse their rebellious ways.

Things haven't changed all that much. Today, our churches shrink from strong messages of repentance, judgment, and the fear of God. We think of ourselves as a much kinder, gentler generation whose focus is on Love, Peace, and Blessings. While we may acknowledge the severe side of the personality of God, we just don't think it applies to us. I call them "feel good ministries" because that's what their messages are about.

When a strong minister of God stands up to preach righteousness and calls the church to repent, we dismiss him just like the Israelites did way back then. Our money, on the other hand, will go to preachers that will tell us what we want to hear. As a matter of fact, the Bible says we will <u>heap</u> up teachers to ourselves, having itching ears.

But there comes a time when God has had enough.

Judgment is always preceded by fearless prophets and courageous men of God who do not care what anyone thinks of them but who will faithfully deliver a hard message to call us to repentance before it is too late.

And then it comes.

> *"He, that being often reproved hardeneth his neck, shall suddenly be destroyed, and that without remedy." Proverbs 29:1*

I believe that there has been a major shift from the dispensation of Jeremiah, who cried out for the people of God to repent, to the dispensation of Zechariah, who spoke of restoration. But restoration does not come without people who will throw themselves on the altar with broken-hearted repentance for how we have failed God, and who will cry out from the depths of their hearts for revival and mercy.

And therein lies the test.

A plumbline is being set, and a line is being drawn in the sand -- you will be on one side of the line or the other. These are the last days, and we are faced with one last call.

He has given us a space of time to repent, but we have not repented. We have magnified and promoted our desire for a Gospel of Love and Blessings but have left off to fear the Lord. We celebrate our ease in the Gospel with songs of love, consoling messages without conviction, and prophets who lead us away from the suffering of the Cross to the promises of prosperity.

The line is being drawn as we sing and dance, but very few notice. Once the line is set, however, we may find ourselves on the wrong side of it and watch as God raises up stones in our place.

Kingdom of God Within

> *"And when he was demanded of the Pharisees, when the kingdom of God should come, he answered them and said, The kingdom of God cometh not with observation: Neither shall they say, Lo here! or, lo there! for, behold, the kingdom of God is within you." Luke 17:20,21*

They just didn't get it. But then, they still don't get it, even today.

The kingdom of God is not manifested in outward appearances of church or religious traditions, no matter how venerated and established. It is something that is birthed inside you when the glory of God is revealed to you at that glorious moment of Salvation.

How do you explain to someone what it is like to feel the glory of God fill your soul when they are stuck on measuring faith with a carnal yardstick? How do you picture for them what it is like to have that deep, personal relationship with the Lord – a relationship that, for the first time, is not a one-way street but is an entrance into a world of the Spirit of God that has literally transformed you from the inside out?

It is like describing the color red to a blind man.

There are no staid ceremonies, no religious ordinations, nor any outward signs when you cross over that threshold from Death unto Life. Sin is invisible, and when that burden is lifted off your soul and the Spirit of God bursts within you with new life, it is not something that you can observe with your eyes. It is a Light that floods your soul that makes you know that you have been born again.

When David danced before the Lord and gloried in His presence, Michal, his wife, disdained him. She was the daughter of Saul, who represented the carnal church, and she could not see the glory of God that David exulted in. Instead of seeing something wonderful, she measured her husband's actions against the established decorum of the old ways of doing things. She just couldn't see the kingdom of God that was within him.

Even Jesus, who after he had done so many miracles and spoke with the anointed power of God, was accused of being a devil because He did not do things according to the traditional ways of the church. He answered the Pharisees by pointing out that because they would not repent, they could not understand. Oh, if they could have just looked beyond the religious wall they had constructed and acknowledged the obvious moving of the Spirit of God!

How about you? Do you measure things according to your church's traditional ways of doing things, and like Michal and the Pharisees, miss seeing the Spirit of God at work? Do you measure someone's salvation by whether or not it fits your church's doctrine?

The kingdom of God is within you and cannot be viewed through the windows of a dead church.

Be careful the next time you accuse someone of not being saved because they don't go to church on the same day you do, or because they believe in a Sinner's Prayer and you don't, or because they have a different take on what it means to serve the Lord. It may be that you are looking for the kingdom of God in a carnal religion and are blinded to the kingdom of God that is within.

It's not something you can see with your eyes; it's an experience.

Your Name is Written There!

Have you ever wanted to see your name in lights, featured in a movie, or a character in a famous novel?

That started me thinking about all the people mentioned in the Bible. Everybody has heard about the more famous (or infamous) ones ... Adam & Eve, Moses, David, Paul, John the Baptist, Pharaoh, Esther, and so on. But really, just to have my name mentioned once or twice in the greatest book in the world would be a huge honor. So, I went through a couple of Bible dictionaries to find the lesser-known people and what they did to earn such an "honorable mention." Here are just a few:

Abi: the mother of King Hezekiah (II Kings 18:2)

Gibea: a grandson of Caleb (I Chronicles 2:49)

Nahbi: a spy from Naphtali sent out by Moses (Num. 13:14)

Shiphrah: one of the Hebrew midwives who risked their lives to save the Hebrew boy babies (Exodus 1:15-21)

Hashbadana: a man who stood by Ezra as he read the law to the people (Neh. 8:4)

Jehudi: one who sat with the princes in Jehoiakim's court and who secured from Baruch the prophecies of Jeremiah and read them to the king (Jer. 36: 14, 21)

Mibhar: one of David's mighty men (I Chron. 11:38)

Eutychus: a youth of Troas who, while listening to Paul preach, was overcome with sleep and fell out of the third-story window. Paul restored him to life. (Acts 20: 9)

Patrobas: a Roman Christian to whom Paul sent greetings (Rom. 16:14)

Rei: one who did not join Adonijah in his rebellion against David (I Kings 1:8)

Secundus: a Thessalonian Christian, otherwise unknown, who with several others had preceded Paul to Troas (Acts 20:4)

This is just a small list. Even though they only have a one-liner in the Bible, some of their actions just to get listed are pretty impressive - a spy, a mighty man in a great army, a law-defying midwife, a citizen of Rome who was a Christian, a loyal subject who did not commit treason against his king.

But there is one book greater than even the Bible: The Book of Life. If your name is written there, Jesus Himself wrote it in with His blood. You didn't have to auction your name off to benefit some non-profit cause in some dark novel. I think that would be the best book of all to have my name mentioned in.

> *"He that overcometh, the same shall be clothed in white raiment; and I will not blot out his name out of the book of life, but I will confess his name before my Father, and before his angels." Rev. 3:5*

Letter from Chris

I'd like to share a letter with you that I received from a young teenager in the United Arab Emirates. I've edited it in some places for clarity's sake:

"Truly, we are in the end-times. The recent disaster in America all proves that. I did not really think that the moral values in America were diminishing, but after Katrina struck New Orleans and the surrounding places, instead of a relief effort, I saw looting, gunfire, etc.

How come "the big brother " who told the good news of Christ to all the world, their moral values are gone? I love America more than my home country, not because of materialistic gains, but instead of the glory of God in its churches, the fire that spread to all nations, which opened the eyes of many nations to the true Gospel, which also opened my eyes. All these I wrote because I love the U.S., not because I hate. I am just opening my heart to you.

I think that majority of people out there have no faith. If you want to see miracles come to my home country India. A leper was healed instantly near my home in India when a group of brothers, after a meeting, were going back to their home and saw a leper in the street. They asked him, "Do you know Jesus?" He replied, "NO." They again asked him, "Do you believe that Jesus can heal you?" He said, "Yes." They prayed in Jesus' name and asked him to open his hands, and he was made whole. His disease left him.

Last year, a dead child was raised back to life. Aids patients were healed. There have been so many miracles around the world.

If anybody has a heart like the disciples of Christ, he can change many to Christ. Love captures the heart."

My answer back to him was:

"Unfortunately, you are right. America was founded on the Gospel of Jesus Christ. The early forefathers came here to establish a country where God would be the glory of the land. That foundation was so strong that it lasted for hundreds of years, but we have now become a very secular country. Slowly but surely, God's predominance has been pushed off the table and is now an unwelcome guest.

You are correct about the horrible things that happened in New Orleans. I am told that earlier this year, a prophet here in America said that God would "cleanse" New Orleans. He has done exactly that. New Orleans is a wicked city, far worse than even San Francisco. Judgment was inevitable. The way these people acted has shocked everyone. Had a tragedy like that struck any other city, you would have seen the entire population of the city come together. Not so in New Orleans. Nevertheless, look at the outpouring of support that rose up around the country. Millions of dollars, truckloads of food and supplies, and housing opened up in almost every city around. There are still Christian roots deep in the American soul.

But Satan has been hard at work for a long time, and he is gaining ground. His first objective was to dumb down the churches and settle them into a spiritual slumber. The American church is no longer on-fire like it once was. Because we have not seen persecution since we left Europe, we no longer feel the need for battle, and our edge, once so sharp, is now so dull that we cannot feel the cutting edge of the reproof of the Word of God.

Once the sharp edge of the Gospel became dull, it was easy to convince Christians that we no longer needed to <u>fear</u> the Lord, just <u>love</u> Him. Once the fear of the Lord is removed, lukewarmness follows, and sin is hard on its heels. And judgment will follow sin.

I fear that the prophecy in Isaiah 18 refers to America because "Unto whom much is given, much is required." America was given more light than any other country but has now given itself over to a secular Gospel that has no power and no teeth. That is why we see so few miracles in America, but such a display of the power of God in foreign countries. There are still some miracles here. I have prayed over people who had leukemia, AIDS, and other diseases, and they were healed instantly, but those miracles have become fewer and farther between. In Mark 6, Jesus experienced the same thing when he could do no miracles in his home country and <u>marveled</u> because of their unbelief.

When I was in the Philippines, the contrast was overwhelming. There, people are starving for more of God, crying out for revival, and have opened their hearts to receive whatever God has for them. The power of God was so thick in those services; it was like walking in a fog. No matter how hard I preached God's Word, they wanted more.

It is the same in Africa. They have pleaded for me to bring that same strong message to them there, but here in America, that message is met with yawns because we do not feel it applies to us. We are not hungry enough to seek His face so our hearts can be open to the Truth.

Yes, love captures the heart, but it is the fear of God that brings us to a place of righteousness where our hearts can be captured by the Love of God. I fear that we have swayed too far from that concept to ever understand and come back to that place in God that we once held.

Your Brother,

Dale"

And this from a 14-yr. old kid in a foreign country. We should be ashamed. Hopefully, we will be convicted to pray, like Nehemiah and Daniel did, for the sins of our people that have taken us so far from God.

One More Night with the Frogs

"And Moses said unto Pharaoh, Glory over me: when shall I intreat for thee, and for thy servants, and for thy people, to destroy the frogs from thee and thy houses, that they may remain in the river only?

And he said, Tomorrow. And he said, Be it according to thy word: that thou mayest know that there is none like unto the LORD our God." Exodus 8:9,10

Oh, that's just great! One more night with the frogs.

You know, for the life of me, I have never been able to figure this out. Why wait until the next day? Am I missing something here? I'll bet I'm not the only one who hasn't figured this out. Moses thought it was important enough to include in the Book of Exodus for all of us to read, so maybe he wondered also.

Could Pharaoh have been so stubborn that his pride would not let him admit how bad things really were? There were frogs in their clothes, in their homes, and in the streets. When they woke up in the morning, they were pulling frogs out from between the bed sheets. When they put their hand in their pockets to pull out a dollar, they got a real greenback. When they took a spoonful of soup, they had to kiss a frog. They were everywhere.

Didn't Pharaoh think it was bad enough to get rid of them right away?

No, let's wait until tomorrow so no one can see that we are really bothered by this. We can put up with these slimy intruders for a few more hours just so we can keep up appearances. After all, we don't want anyone to see us admit that we were wrong.

How stupid is that?

We may sit back and point the finger at Pharaoh, but do we not have frogs in our own lives that we just simply don't want to admit to? We see them in our government, in our churches, and in our jobs. There are frogs everywhere, including in our daily habits. We're quick to point them out in others (in some cases, we figure our bosses or our politicians are the frogs), but we are loath to admit how our own lives are infested with them.

So, we put on appearances and tell ourselves that we will get rid of them tomorrow. But when tomorrow comes and the frogs are dead, we often harden our hearts and get ready for the lice. And so it goes.

Pride often keeps us from seeing a true picture of what trouble really is. When we refuse to give in to what we know in our hearts is causing so much trouble in our lives, we fail to see that trouble as the mercy of God.

God uses trouble to take the trouble out of our lives. When we refuse to hearken to His reproof, we send ourselves back into the fire. If we finally humble ourselves and acknowledge our sins, God can then bring us to a place of deliverance.

I believe that Hurricane Katrina and disasters like that were just like that plague of frogs. If we acknowledge that God controls the wind and the seas, we might pause to reflect upon how vulnerable we are to the sovereignty of God. If, on the other hand, we write it off as just another natural occurrence, we stand the chance of setting ourselves up for what is coming next.

Just as the frogs in Egypt didn't just dissolve into thin air -- they had to gather them up into heaps and live with the stench to remind them of what they had just been through – so will we also be reminded for months to come of the devastation that only took hours to fall upon us.

Perhaps God is giving us time to consider our ways.

One Thing

> *"And, behold, one came and said unto him, Good Master, what good thing shall I do, that I may have eternal life?"* Matthew 19:17

Let's see now, what can we pick? Surely there is one thing that we can find that will secure us a place in Heaven. We just have to figure that one thing out, and we're in!

You know, as stupid as that sounds, I actually tried to do that once. What could I do to make sure that there would be no question anymore that I would make it into Heaven and escape the horrors of Hell?

I thought and thought, and I realized that it was going to take a lot more than one single thing, but I wanted to settle this issue once and for all, so I came up with what I thought would really lock me in. I started praying for God to reveal how big He was in comparison to how small I was.

Simple, I figured. If I could just get a glimpse of the incredible greatness of God, I would fall down in so much fear of God that I would never fall into sin ever again for the rest of my life.

Well, that sounded pretty good to me, so I prayed and fasted until my tongue was dragging on the floor. It was getting pretty tough, but still no answer from the Lord ... until the 4th day.

I was trudging along in prayer (and I mean trudging), wondering if maybe I had shot just a little too high on this thing because I wasn't getting anywhere, and it was getting harder and harder when suddenly the Lord answered. It was so quick that it was over before it began, but in that briefest of instants, I caught a fleeting glimpse of the awesome, unbelievable, eternal power of God. He wasn't just <u>this</u> powerful or <u>that</u> powerful ... He was <u>ALL</u> powerful!

I stood there, stumbling from the overwhelming shock of it. It was too much for my little dirt-of-the-ground brain to grasp, and I realized that, had He extended that brief instant even a millisecond longer, I probably would have exploded from the awesome power of just the sight of it.

And yet, there I was, still standing there, locked into my own fleshly ways.

Well, I wasn't too sure that was really fair. After all, I had fasted for days, and I was still me. I hadn't changed into some kind of supernatural, Super Christian.

Nuts. I guess there just isn't any quick and instant easy way to do this. It didn't matter how great God was. I was still going to have to work at it.

And if I thought I could just do one thing so I could walk in the depths of the fear of God, I was mistaken. It was going to take prayer, lots of it, and I was going to have to keep on praying and fasting while I was still here on Earth.

I imagine the rich, young ruler in Matthew 19 felt pretty much the same way. You couldn't just snap your fingers, and, bingo, you were locked in so you could go on with the rest of your life. No shortcuts to Heaven.

Jesus didn't ask him to do any tricks, roll over and bark, give canned goods to the poor, or wear a Jesus t-shirt to work. Jesus asked him to surrender his heart, and that was the one thing he was not willing to give up.

There is no doctrine that will save your soul; there's no church membership that will give you a "Get In Free" card; there's no display of holiness that will win you points with God. Only the Blood of Jesus Christ can pay the price for your sins, and only complete surrender to God will secure you a place in Heaven. You've got to be broken and yielded to pick up your cross and follow Him. Nothing else counts.

> *"Thou meetest him that rejoiceth and worketh righteousness, those that remember thee in thy ways: ... in those is continuance, and we shall be saved."*
> *Isaiah 64:5*

I'm Back

Boy, is it good to be back in Texas! A month in Africa is a long time to eat rice and beans, take showers with a bucket and a scoop, and drink Nescafe's imitation coffee out of a package. It did not take me long after I got off the plane to get myself a real cup of coffee and go find a McDonald's.

There are some other differences that I have had to deal with also.

Americans are immersed in luxuries that Africans cannot even imagine in their life of desperation. They are so used to being so poor for so long that their despair is worn like a piece of old clothing. But that's exactly the place where great moves of God are found.

I have preached thousands of messages over the years across Africa, and every message was spontaneous and in the Spirit. Time and time again, the Lord would give me the passage to preach from only minutes before I was supposed to stand up. And even then, I was rarely able to see what the message was going to be about. But the Lord would unfold the message as I spoke. Most of the time, the Lord would be giving me next thing to say as the translator was delivering the last thing I said. Talk about being spoon-fed!

How sad that our sophisticated pastors here think they must prepare their sermons for Sunday. They have forgotten how to trust God for the message, and as a result, their messages become dry and uninspired.

There was a thick anointing of the Spirit of God that was palpable in every service we had over there. Now, for many of us here in the States, we have no idea what that is like. Then again, Africans have no idea what our services are like, either. They cannot imagine services that are boring and liturgical in nature or sweet and social like what is found in so many of our churches here. They thrive on the raw power of the Holy Ghost and immerse themselves in that anointing for 4 to 6 hours – and yet, it feels like only 30 minutes have passed.

I would come out of some of those services after having ministered for over 2 hours, not able to walk in a straight line. At one service, I had to be helped outside because I was floating from the anointing. At other times, it felt like my hands were dripping with oil from praying over these people.

There was power over there that we only dream about because there is a hunger there that we don't know about. We are too full and satisfied. We are rich and increased with goods and do not realize that we are poor and miserable and blind. We are the

Church of the Laodiceans. We think we are still God's City on a Hill, the light that shines to the rest of the world, but those days are over, and God's attention is shifting to those who are desperate for Him. We are not desperate enough to cry out for revival with the level of passion that He will hear, and we are not willing to pay the high price that God requires for Him to move.

I went to church yesterday -- my first service since I've been back – and everyone was so glad to see me and talked about how happy I must be to be home again. The pastor mentioned that everyone would just love to hear the stories sometime. It was as if I had just come back from a vacation to the Grand Canyon. How nice. But I could feel an unrest and a stirring in the Spirit that was not good, as if the Lord was offended. It was like coming out of the real world and walking into a detergent commercial where everything is so nice and clean … and naïve.

How do you make them see the difference? You can't. Their hearts are not ready to receive that level of depth because they aren't desperate enough.

> *I will go and return to my place, till they acknowledge their offence, and seek my face: in their affliction they will seek me early. Hosea 5:15*

Gideon's Call

> *"Now therefore go to, proclaim in the ears of the people, saying, Whosoever is fearful and afraid, let him return and depart early from mount Gilead."*
> *Judges 7:3*

I am reminded when I read the passages about Gideon that the Apostle Paul wrote that perilous times would come to the church in the last days. While we expect that the peril will come from the Antichrist or something dark and devious, the truth is that Paul didn't really elaborate on where the peril would come from. He does, however, make several references in the ensuing passage to the church, or so-called established church.

The story of Gideon is a story of deliverance to a church that is fallen and has been defeated by the world. Like the Israelites, we have not hearkened to the prophets that God has sent, so as a result, we are oppressed in our own land by the Midianites of this world. They have taken over our schools, our media, our marketplace, and yes, even our churches. They have left us nothing in a land that was once wholly given to God.

What happened? The same thing that happened to the children of Israel -- we forgot God.

One generation ago, things were vastly different. Just as the generation before Gideon had a much different walk than their fathers had with Joshua, so our grandfathers' generation had a much different walk with God than we do. But like Gideon's generation, we have fallen away from that old-fashioned fear of God.

Weren't there warnings? Oh yes, but we decided that we were too sophisticated to heed them, so we allowed ourselves to slip into a worldly church and allowed the Midianites in.

Where were the strong men of God who had the courage to stand up and declare war on the enemy? Good question. All the ones that I've ever read about from the last generation are dead. Anyone who has stood up in the midst of this last "churchy" generation has been dismissed as "judgmental."

Guess what? They are absolutely correct. They <u>are</u> judgmental. Unfortunately, this generation shrinks from judgment and the fear of the Lord and has reaped the results.

There is a Gideon generation about to rise, but it will not come out of our church denominations. As a matter of fact, it will probably be looked at askew from our pulpits simply because so few have enough guts to make a stand for righteousness. If they did, they would have already done so, but instead, they have settled for a comfortable "church as usual" – no price, no confrontations, no battles, and no victory. They are afraid of war.

Not only are those whom the Lord will raise up NOT afraid of war, they will charge into the smoke of battle.

Like Gideon, they are tired of hearing about the miracles that happened in the past – they want to see them now! They are sick and tired of church – they want to see the real thing. They are tired of hearing excuses for a dead church with boring services – they want to feel the excitement of the power of the Holy Ghost. They are tired of seeing Christians hide in the dens of the rocks for fear of the world, society, and the established church – they are ready to stand up and fight for an outpouring of the Holy Spirit and to hell with any foul spirit that stands in their way!

They are ready to fight for the kingdom of God against all odds, against all sense and persuasion, and against all resistance from the church world. They know that perilous times are here – and they know where it is coming from. They know that the deck is stacked against them, but they don't care.

If you are fearful and afraid, then just like in Gideon's call, just go home and get out of the way. We are here for battle, and we shall fight for the righteousness of God and to restore the presence of the Holy Spirit in our churches no matter what stands in the way.

And we shall prevail because the battle is not of flesh and blood, but victory is of the Lord.

False Revival

> *"So, he came to the king. And the king said unto him, Micaiah, shall we go against Ramoth-gilead to battle, or shall we forbear? And he answered him, Go, and prosper: for the LORD shall deliver it into the hand of the king."* I Kings 22:15

Sometimes I feel like I have more questions than answers, and sometimes I am left wondering why the things I see do not line up with the things I feel. I guess that's where the proverb comes in that it is the glory of God to conceal a thing, but the honor of kings is to search out a matter.

Often, something sounds so good on the surface but doesn't feel right in your guts, and you wonder why.

For instance, I keep hearing about the coming "breakthrough" revival that is just about to hit this area in which I live, specifically through Assemblies of God. Many Christians are excited about the coming prospects. You can hear it in their voices as they tell you about all the prophesies that have been spoken over them and the visitations from other revivalists who feel like this area is a "magnet for God."

They will tell you that they have even gone on a 40-day fast for this revival. Of course, they didn't really fast for 40 days; they just had a lot of people go on a lot of tiny fasts for a <u>period</u> of 40 days. They talk about the all-night prayer meetings they've had for revival. They don't tell you that they didn't actually pray all night – they just had a bunch of people take a lot of little time slots <u>throughout</u> the night.

They talk about getting right with God and getting "realigned" or "shifting to correction", but nothing is mentioned about broken-hearted repentance and weeping before God. Instead, we hear about the wonderful party they had at the revival meeting.

Gee, it all sounds so good, and who would dare to say anything disparaging about it? But you know, the more I hear about it, the more that something seems missing.

So I back up a bit and give the same sarcastic answer as Micaiah did, "Go and prosper."
"Hope everything is beautiful."
"You go, girl!"
"Good luck."
"Hope you make it!"

In my heart, however, what they are spilling out just doesn't feel the same as what they try to make it sound like. What these people are calling for is a party with all the balloons, but I hear nothing about the desperation that the Word of God requires for revival.

If they are afraid to even speak the severe words that call for deep, broken repentance, then do they really think that their churchy, substitute phrases will pierce through to people's hearts?

If all they will fast is for a day or so, and all they will pray is an hour or so, then it doesn't sound to me like they are serious. You can quote all the so-called "fair-haired boy" prophesies that you want, but I don't see that kind of "pretty prophesies" in the Bible without a price being paid somewhere by somebody.

Any revival that comes without a crucified price from the people of God is superficial at best and will not come with any substance. Lest we forget, the altar of God is not a place of singing and dancing but of blood, sacrifice, and death.

I do not see broken hearts that are desperate for a return to righteousness so they can have an outpouring of the Holy Ghost. Neither do I see people that are cut to the heart for lost souls that are on their way to an everlasting Hell.

Until I see that, like Micaiah, I remain unimpressed.

Sure of Salvation

How do you explain to someone how to be sure of their salvation? There is no more important question in life – you have to know completely without any shadow of doubt that you are saved. You cannot guess on this one. You cannot hope that you <u>probably</u> are, and you cannot take a chance that maybe God is going to let you in. You have to know.

While faith is the substance of things hoped for, and it is something that God does insert into our core being, it is also something that needs to be absolutely confirmed, otherwise, you stand a good chance of becoming a stark, raving heretic. Fifty years ago, I heard there were 60,000 different religions – there's got to be over 100,000 by now. Which one are you going to pick? They all think that they are the one that is right and that everyone else is going to Hell.

I always point to the Spirit of God. The Apostle John said that the way you can tell is by the Spirit that God has given us. (1 John 3:24) Well, I reckon that means that you have to be able to feel it. If you can't feel it, maybe it's because you ain't got it.

Now, I'm not talking about experiencing emotional highs and getting excited over singing songs in church. I'm talking about something external, outside the group of wild and excited dancers, the hand-wavers, and hallelujah-shouters. I'm talking about the real thing – that personal touch from the Lord when you reach past your flesh and touch the Throne of God. (If you don't know what I'm talking about, we need to talk.)

And yet, millions of people hang onto their dead religion because that is what they have been taught to believe. My question is not where the Truth lies, but why doesn't everybody get saved? The answer I've gotten from the Lord is that some people care and some people don't. It's as simple as that.

Hmmm. I can grasp that. But my next question is, why don't they care? Don't they realize there is a burning Hell? The answer lies somewhere along the lines of their dismissal of facts that they don't want to face. But even at that, I am still puzzled as to why people will cling so tenaciously to a dead religion.

It has to be a matter of the little choices we make in Life. We will have a tendency to follow our hearts, and if we really don't care about Truth, we will instead choose that which is either more appetizing or more convenient and convince ourselves that it really doesn't matter.

In other words, we just really don't care.

Where's the Beef?

(Old Wendy's Hamburgers commercial)

We all want the same thing ... well, pretty much all of us. Everybody wants to go to Heaven and be right with God. And the ones that don't are just hoping that at least there is no Hell. The problem is that we want to go on our terms. That makes it a tricky issue. Who's to say which the right way is?

I have an answer for that. It is in 1st John. We know we are in Him by the Spirit that He has given us. (1 John 3:24)

You would think that would make it simple. Either you got it, or you don't. But now we have to debate over how you determine if you have the Spirit or not. (Scheesh! Does it ever end?)

To that, all I can say is that if you have to figure it out, you don't have it.

But there are those who think they feel the Spirit every time they feel a gust of wind when they're singing in services. I see them twirling around and bouncing up and down and getting all happy. Well, at least that's better than handling snakes just to prove you're in the Spirit.

But where's the beef?

I believe that the Spirit of God responds in a very real way to worship. But is that all there is? When we go home after a rousing service, what happens then? After the euphoria wears off, are we left in the same old flesh, just waiting for our next fix? There has to be something more.

Real depth in God comes from elements that are not associated with singing and dancing. It's the more serious side of the Gospel that brings us to that secret place of the Most High that pulls us out of our flesh and into a deeper walk with God. The suffering of the Cross is supposed to be manifest in our lives. (And please, I'm not talking about whipping yourself or anything weird like that.)

What about a crucified walk? Or how about being grieved for lost souls? Or allowing yourself to go through the fire, or letting God take you through valleys to strip away your flesh?

I could go on and on. I know you've read about this stuff, but not many want to think about that side of the Gospel. You see, that's the stuff that makes a real Christian -- the walks in the valleys, not the experiences on the mountaintops.

To put it succinctly, we don't want to face our own death. And yet, that is exactly where the Lord wants to take us if we are ever going to have power in God. A friend once told me, "God isn't trying to change you. He's trying to kill you!" Amen. But that ol' flesh just doesn't want to die.

It takes serious depths in the Word of God and desperate prayer to bring us to the point where we are willing to allow God to break our hearts and strip us down. Without that, however, we are just like kindergarteners running around on the playground, having a good time, but not going anywhere.

Revivals are birthed in heartbreak and sacrifice -- not the instant, "cheap 'n' easy" version that echoes the Lottery mentality of this generation. There is a price for everything in God.

God is looking for those with a serious dedication to serve the Lord and stand against the powers of darkness. That comes from a battle-hardened determination to overcome all things and carry the Cross.

It may not be as much fun as we'd like, but it is the path that leads to Calvary.

Jacob's Staff

"By faith Jacob, when he was a dying, blessed both the sons of Joseph; and worshipped, leaning upon the top of his staff." Hebrews 11:21

Chapter 11 of Hebrews is one of my favorite chapters. I like hearing about people who had that grit in their souls to reach for more than just plodding through life. Many of them believed in the Word of God so much that they were willing to suffer terribly to uphold it and to keep it intact. That kind of stuff always has a strong effect on me.

This scripture about Jacob, however, has always puzzled me. Most of the time, when I don't get something, I just move on and figure that if the Lord wants to reveal something to me, He will. If He doesn't, then I'll just keep on reading rather than try to wrestle something with my own understanding.

But I just cannot help wondering, where did Paul get this stuff about leaning on the staff? Not that it is a big deal or anything, but I'd just like to know.

Maybe Paul is just trying to fill in the story. Let's face it, he can get long-winded sometimes, so maybe this is just to spice it up and bring the picture to life. That's something we all do, so I can relate to that. I mean, what's interesting about some old man who can barely stand up praying a blessing over his two grandsons? Maybe the staff thing is just there to make it more interesting to read.

Then again, maybe he got it from some other book, like the Alternate History of Israel or some such thing. I always hear about all these "other" texts whenever someone wants to get around something they don't like in the Bible, so maybe there's a bunch of these alternate readings lying around somewhere, and Paul, who we know was very learned, got this from some other text. After all, what's the big deal? One text is as good as another, isn't it?

Of course, there's always the possibility that he got it directly from God ...

The problem with that is that if he got it straight from the Lord, then there must be something important about this staff thing. Maybe it is not so easily dismissed as we might flippantly think. Just because I can't see the significance of this old man leaning upon his staff doesn't necessarily mean that there isn't some underlying importance to it that I don't see. I think I'll just leave it word for word the way Paul spelled it out.

You know, I have no idea what the answers are, but I wouldn't dare dismiss this seemingly unimportant detail about Jacob's staff. Someday, the Lord may show us something absolutely incredible about it that we would have never thought of. Until then, I will leave the Word of God intact.

I just wonder why so many scholars do not have the same fear of God and reverence for His Word when they have produced today's modern translations. Maybe they're just smarter than the rest of us.

Prepared Messages

> *"And he that keepeth his commandments dwelleth in him, and he in him. And hereby we know that he abideth in us, by the Spirit which he hath given us."*
> 1John 3:24

I'm stuck on the importance of this Scripture.

After all the debates are finished and all the theological arguments are expired, it always boils down to this one thing: are you in the Spirit or not? If you have the Spirit of God resting upon your life, the rest doesn't really matter, does it?

And contrariwise, if you don't have the Spirit of God on you, it doesn't matter either. What good is it to know volumes of theological doctrine, have a wall full of diplomas and certifications, and not be in the Spirit of God?

Now this will seem to be a bedrock of simplicity to those who know what it means to feel the Spirit of God resting upon them, but for those who run in theological circles, it is a mystery that they can only explain away by falling back on religious tradition and carnal analysis.

To me, it is a bottom-line argument – either you got it, or you don't.

This has never been more evident than these last few weeks that I have been back from my last trip to Africa. After going through almost 40 services where the Spirit of God was flowing like oil in every service, I came back to what can only be described as a spiritual desert. It was like going from fire to ice.

There we flowed under the anointing; here we trudge through by rote. Services there sometimes lasted for four or five hours but felt like they only lasted for a short time; here, the services are clipped after an hour or so but feel like they last forever. Could we be missing something? I'm telling you, the people over there wonder what is wrong with us when they hear that our services only last for a couple of hours.

Our preachers here have allowed their biblical education to convince them that they must "prepare" their sermons all week long so they can shuffle through their notes on the pulpit and deliver their didactic lecture for 30 minutes. We leave church dry and parched, and ten minutes after we pass through the doorway, we have forgotten what it was about. Boy, that really changed our lives, didn't it?

I have never believed in preparing my message. The Lord gives me the passage that He is going to use just minutes before I get up to preach, and then I watch as He unfolds the message and develops it. I hear the message at the same time that everyone else does. But you know what? When God is the one giving the message, it changes lives.

I listen to pastors claim that they are not confined by their denomination, but all I ever hear from them is the rattling inside their denominational box. It is all they know, and it seems that they are afraid to trust God enough to step outside it and let God deliver the message that His people need to hear. Their trust lies somewhere in the pages of their disheveled notes, not in the anointed leading of the Holy Ghost.

Up until now, I have never made this a pointed argument, but lately, the Lord has been dealing with me about the lack of trust by our preachers to just yield and let God take over. Is it any wonder that so many people are tired of church services and are looking for something more than the same old dry sermons that they can hear no matter which church they attend?

Pastors had better be careful because His sheep hear His voice, and another they will not follow. If you don't get out of the way and let God take over, they will hear His voice somewhere else, and you will be left with the goats.

Touch the Cross

"If thou wert pure and upright; surely now he would awake for thee, and make the habitation of thy righteousness prosperous. Though thy beginning was small, yet thy latter end should greatly increase." Bildad the Shuhite, (Job 8:6)

"...For unto you it is given in the behalf of Christ, not only to believe on him, but also to suffer for his sake." Paul, (Philippians 1:29)

There has been a shift in our view of the personality of God. I noticed it taking hold of the evangelical church world about 30 years ago, and it has established itself more firmly ever since.

The old-fashioned view of a God of judgment was mollified to one of a kinder, gentler God who was more attuned to a loving relationship with His children. The old brush arbor revivalists were considered too hard in their outlook, mocked in Hollywood films, and brushed aside as narrow-minded zealots who did not understand the mercy of God. We assumed that we had a better understanding of God because we are somehow more enlightened.

We shifted our focus to the blessings, the love and mercy, and the goodness of God. Yes, judgment was still there but was more relegated to the shadows off-stage than out in the spotlight. The Fear of God, although undeniably written in the Word of God, was analytically digested and has been presented as being more by the precept of men (Isaiah 29:13) than the emotionally charged issue of actual dread and fear (Isaiah 8:13). God is now our Daddy.

Because there was no momentous outpouring of the Holy Spirit in recent memory, we, like the Israelites of Sinai, felt that Moses had taken too long to come down from the mountain, so we've fashioned our own gods that have supposedly delivered us out of Egypt.

Seems to work pretty well. It feels much better, and it is much more palatable than walking around under a cloud of intense holiness as our forefathers did. After all, it makes much more sense to the carnal mind. If you get saved, God will love you and pour out His unconditional Love all over you. No more dark valleys to walk through, no more refining fire to strip away your flesh, and no more sufferings of the Cross to bear.

It made sense to Bildad the Shuhite.

But not to Paul.

We are inundated with an easy Gospel that promises a wonderful time in Jesus. We proclaim that there will be a great revival soon, and we sing and dance to the rhythm of the message, but we have not considered the price. Our pastors who have taken the pulpits in the last 30-some-odd years have regurgitated the message they heard in Bible College and are not even aware that something is missing. But hey, it sure feels good, doesn't it?

So we continue to sing and dance and line up for someone to touch us so we can fall down on the floor in euphoria, but we never notice our lack of depth and brokenness, nor do we consider that old crucified walk that our fathers have trod to establish the Church.

We want to touch the Cross, but not bear it.

Meaningless Hope

This morning I received two very different emails from different parts of the world that made me realize the power of hope that only the Word of God can bring us.

The first message came from a 26-year-old girl in Ethiopia. In broken English, she asked me to pray for her and help her with advice because she was struggling with "meaningless hope."

That may seem contradictory, but to someone down at the bottom of a dark well of despair, the faint glimmer of hope can seem more like a faded mirage than something you can actually cling to. You begin to think that the things you had based your faith on were no more real than wishful thinking. If God was really there, you wonder, and if He really cared about you, then why has He left you down in the bottom of this abyss with no hope of getting out?

As you crouch down there, you hear those whispers that tell you that not only are you the only one who has gone through this, but no one else really understands, and nobody cares.

Sound familiar?

My heart felt broken for this girl because I know what she is going through, and I know many others that have experienced the same thing. It's part of the path of the Cross that God leads us down so we can learn how to reach up past the darkness and touch the Throne of God.

But how can I reach all the way to Ethiopia to help this girl?

Then I received another email, this one from another part of the world. It was a Yahoo E-Card that simply said, "You really lifted my spirit. Thank you." I looked at the name and the address but didn't recognize either. Who is this guy? How did I lift his spirits? Was it something I wrote that made its way to him through some email chain? Did he hear a radio message in one of the countries we broadcast from? He didn't say. Just simply, "You really lifted my spirit. Thank you." Somehow the Spirit of the Lord had flowed through unknown channels to reach him with something that he really needed.

Both of these messages came around the same time, and I couldn't help but wonder about how connected they both were.

Hope comes from faith in God's promises, but it is ignited only when the Word is brought forth under the anointing of the Holy Ghost. A Word preached in the "letter" without the anointing of the Spirit will kill hope, as it says in 2nd Corinthians 3:6, but when His Word is brought forth in the Spirit, it carries a light within it to bring hope even to the darkest corners of your despair. How important it is for us to edify one another in the Spirit of God!

The Holy Spirit travels in ways that we cannot see nor understand, and it can reach deeper than we can ever know. The faithfulness of just one word spoken in the Spirit can pierce walls that no other force can and can reach down to the bottom of a well to bring hope that is a ray of salvation to those who have given up on everything else.

Meaningless hope? Only when it does not rest upon God.

"And hope maketh not ashamed; because the love of God is shed abroad in our hearts by the Holy Ghost which is given unto us." Romans 5:5

Desired to Make One Wise

> *"And when the woman saw that the tree was good for food, and that it was pleasant to the eyes, and a tree to be desired to make one wise, she took of the fruit thereof, and did eat..."* Genesis 3:6

Well, she ate it all right, but it sure didn't make her wise. As a matter of fact, that was about the stupidest thing she could have done.

A lot of folks have eaten off that same tree. They've learned a whole bunch of stuff about nothing, but it sure made them feel like they were smart. And they usually want to make sure you know that, too.

Many years ago, a friend named Norman taught me not to be afraid to say, "I don't know." That was a real knock on the head for me because I thought that the object in Life was that the guy who has the most answers at the end of the game wins.

I began to learn, however, that no matter how much "stuff" I knew, it amounted to nothing. Shucks, all you have to do when you start feeling really smart, is walk outside and look up at the stars. That'll shrink you back down to size again.

But it seems that human nature has an interminable drive to become wise, to learn some new thing, and to feel like you "know" something. Somehow, when we marry that drive with a desire to be righteous, we begin to believe that by learning more about God, the Bible, or the myriad of conspiracies, legends, and theories that we think of as the "inside truth," somehow, it will make us more righteous with God. But all it ever does is manifest itself as spiritual pride – or as the Apostle Paul said, "Knowledge puffeth up; charity edifieth" (1Cor. 8:1).

Paul said he knew nothing but Christ Jesus, and him crucified. Good point, Paul. What else is there?

I will not get to Heaven because I passed some exam at the Judgment Bar, or have a sack full of good works, or because I know more stuff than the other guy. I will only get there by acknowledging that I am a sinner and that I can do nothing, and I know nothing without Jesus Christ. I need to become blind to my own wisdom so that He can lead me with His. I want to be led by the Spirit of God, not by my own.

But to do that, you have to give up on that desire to become wise.

"For as many as are led by the Spirit of God, they are the sons of God." Romans 8:14

Kids

I am worried about our kids because they are growing up in a world that is increasingly corrupted. I remember a time when there were clear distinctions between right and wrong. If you decided to pursue sin, at least you knew you were wrong.

That is quickly eroding from our society today. Everything is relative and can be explained away with our new theories of social interactions and psychological excuses. Sin isn't so bad anymore.

But to stand for righteousness because it is the right thing to do, now that's bad. If you choose to make that stand, then you are quickly labeled as stupidly narrow-minded, unenlightened, or worse, judgmental. It's a tough world out there for someone who wants to be righteous before God.

But I believe that right is right, and wrong is wrong. There are bedrock truths that will stand no matter how you try to get around them.

I often think of the scripture, "Thou shalt not seethe a kid in its mother's milk." Ever wonder about that? Let's face it, the baby goat doesn't know anything – it's dead. And I'm sure the mother isn't aware of who's cooking whom with what. So what's the big deal? It's a victimless crime.

But some things are wrong because they are wrong, and that will never change.

But to understand that, you have to concede to the authority of God. Ahh. There's the rub! We have to humble ourselves to God and acknowledge Him as God over all the Earth. But that means we can't just do whatever we want when we want to do it. That is the same original sin that Satan first manifested when he said he would be like the Most High God. He didn't want to submit.

But what do we offer our kids as a reason to stay righteous before God? There must be more than just intellectual reasons to counteract the powerful urges of the hormones pumping through their systems or the subtle influences of an alluring world of sin. What do we have to offer them?

Telling them that they should believe in God just because we tell them so is not enough. Or telling them that the Bible is wiser than the psycho-babble that explains away sin. Or trying to woo them with a "God loves them, so they should love God" answer. We have to give them something more than that to strengthen their resolve to hold on to the righteousness of God.

For years, I have cried that our churches have become empty shells of what they once used to be. The power is missing. Oh, true, we say and do the same things we always have, but somehow the presence of the power of the Holy Ghost has dissipated into a faded memory of the times when our churches were on fire. We have traded the presence of God for a ventriloquist's doll.

And yet, God is still there, His judgments are still set, and there is still a burning Hell. It's not God that has changed. It's that we have forgotten how to tap into that place in God that once forged our faiths.

The strength to stand in the Spirit of God does not come from believing in God or knowing what is right, or even the specter of Hell. It has to come from the anointing of the Holy Ghost that inhabits our life, manifests itself in church, and fills our souls with glory, but to get there, we have to change our religious ways and return back to a time when we walked with God. The Spirit of God is the only sure remedy for the sickness of sin and temptation.

But we have turned to a more modern perspective and, as a result, have lost the evidence of His presence. All we have to offer are stories of what once was.

And that is not enough.

Debate

> *"When therefore the Lord knew how the Pharisees had heard that Jesus made and baptized more disciples than John, (Though Jesus himself baptized not, but his disciples,) He left Judea, and departed again into Galilee." John 4:1-3*

I noticed that Jesus had a way of detouring around debate. He could have waited for the Pharisees to start their little dog and pony show and then blown them all away. Jesus was not intimidated by them. There would be plenty of time for that later. He chose to leave before controversy took over the real reason why He was there.

The Pharisees, on the other hand, loved debate. There is a religious spirit there that drives us to assert ourselves over the next person just to manifest the dominance of our righteousness. It's as if there is some kind of lust of the flesh that makes us want to charge into the fray on our white stallion, holding up the banner of our self-righteousness.

Man, it gets your blood flowing just thinking about it! Glory, Honor, and Power!

But Jesus didn't do that, did He? While the religious were rattling their theological sabers, He followed a path that led to humility and found a woman by the well in Samaria.

There are times when we are called to stand for righteousness, but never a time when we are called to enter into debate. Even during His most embroiled confrontations with the Pharisees, He was more noted for His famous "drop-the-other-shoe" one-liners than for a heated debate.

He was headed for the Cross, not the Throne. Victory in God does not come through blood and battle. You don't establish your righteousness with knowledge, intellectual dominance, or by being right. It comes through humility and the fear of the Lord.

The cloud and dust of battle mask the true focus of our calling. While strong arguments may make us feel like we have won a victory for the Lord, God's single-minded intentions are to win lost souls –

Something that is forgotten in the heat of battle.

Progression

> *"... Add to your faith virtue; and to virtue knowledge; And to knowledge temperance; and to temperance patience; and to patience godliness; And to godliness brotherly kindness; and to brotherly kindness charity. " 2nd Peter 1:5-7*

Sometimes I feel like I have only gotten halfway through this progression and struggle to grasp the second half.

I have faith, and I know that God is real. It's that touch of the Spirit of God that not only keeps me locked in but drives me toward Him. There's no denying the reality of the presence of God when you are walking in the Spirit.

And I have added to that virtue. I believe in the fear of God, and I know His commandments aren't just good suggestions. I also know that only through the Spirit can I ever have the power to overcome sin, and without it, there's no chance of me being righteous before God, so I nestle in as close as I can to Him for the power to overcome.

To stay in that place of righteousness and virtue, I know I have to read and pray, and that adds knowledge – not knowledge in a theological sense, but the real, vibrant knowledge of God -- His personality, His ways, and a truly personal relationship with Him. You learn as you grow, and as you grow, you see deeper and farther than you could have ever learned on your own.

But sometimes, that increased knowledge and drive to righteousness can lead to spiritual pride and <u>self</u>-righteousness. It has to be tempered with the knowledge that you are still flesh, and it is not through your efforts but by allowing God to take over and flow through your life that you will ever be anything in God. That's a complete reverse of human nature. You will not attain to anything further in God without tempering it with the understanding that you are still just dust and ashes, no matter how much you know.

Then you have to learn patience. Arghh! Learning how to wait upon God and allow Him to take over your life is one of the hardest things you will face in your Christian life. But you have to be patient. If you don't, you will end up launching into the deep without God, and it will only lead to failure.

Ah, but we still haven't arrived, have we? We have to add to that godliness – to be like God. But wait a minute! You mean after all the knowledge, virtue, faith, temperance, and patience, we still haven't become like the Lord?

There's more to being a Christian than being centered on our own lives. Jesus Christ didn't die for himself – He died for others. He extended both his hands far out to the left and right to encompass all of us when He gave His life on the Cross. It's not about us – it's about the death of ourselves and the sacrifice for others. That's what God is like.

Now we're getting close. The next thing is brotherly kindness – that link to the Body of Christ. Instead of lording it over others who have not attained to our level because we "know" so much more than they do, the path to God leads to mercy and kindness to them. It's not about how great you are – it's about how great God is. And that which He has given you, He wants you to give to them. "Freely ye have received; freely give."

Finally, we come to the Cadillac of Christianity – Charity. Charity is the giving of yourself in everything you do, out of love, so that souls will get saved. It is the bottom line of your Faith. It is the whole point of your existence in life. It is the focus of the Cross. It is greater than Faith or Hope. It is the climax of the whole progression that starts from faith.

Jesus Christ is Charity incarnate.

Squirrel

There's a squirrel that lives in the woods across the road that keeps coming over to eat out of my bird feeder. I have popped him pretty good a few times with a BB gun, but he keeps coming back.

What's amazing to me is what he has to go through to get there, and yet he is determined to keep returning. The woods he lives in are of a pretty good size, so there is no lack of food over there – he just wants something more.

I've watched as he runs across the road, up some trees onto a power line, then across that line to the telephone pole, and then across the next line to another pole. He then runs across the next wire to some branches of a tree in our yard, down the tree, across the patio, and up a skinny pole to the bird feeder. You'd think he'd be out of breath by the time he got there, but he keeps coming back, braving the BBs, the prowling cats, and the long trek to get there.

What is it that drives him to push past all obstacles and dangers to eat that birdseed? It's not like there isn't any food in the woods where he lives. No, he has found something in that bird feeder that he hungers for more than anything else. It answers the hunger in his soul, and no matter what it takes, he is willing to overcome all obstacles to get it.

I know how he feels. My heart also hungers for something more.

I guess I could satisfy myself with the convenience of easy religion -- it's all around us, close and convenient, and everybody goes there -- but I want something more. There's an empty spot down in the depths of my heart that hungers for something that only the Spirit of God can fill.

I don't want just a nice church service where you have a pleasant time, fellowship with friends, and leave not quite remembering what the message was about. I want the thunder and lightning of the storm that transforms you and drives you into another world. I want to get hit by the lightning! I want to feel the driving rain of the storm! I want to get soaked to the bone!

Sometimes I wonder if I'm just too intense. Of course, it could be that I'm just plain nuts, but whatever I am, my soul is hungry for something more, and like that squirrel, I would cross Hell itself to find that place in God that my heart is crying out for.

I reckon I'll put the BB gun away, or, better yet, maybe throw out some corn for the little guy.

Balance

My mother used to tell me that everything in life was balanced – everything. She believed that nature would compensate for different people that had physical problems by enhancing their other abilities and senses. Different people had different strengths and weaknesses, and it all balanced out in the end. Even homosexuals, she would point out, made up for their aberration with artistic talents. As a young child growing up in New York City, a lot of the artists and movie stars that I saw seemed pretty weird, so that kind of validated my mother's insight, and I grew up accepting it as a primal truth.

As all teenagers do, I began to analyze life for myself (realizing, of course, that I was smarter than my parents), and began to reach some very different conclusions. Life wasn't quite so balanced as I had been led to believe, not only in physical abilities but also in morality. Some things just simply outweighed others, and not everything or everybody was equal.

When I got saved, the issue became even more complicated. At first, I thought everybody believed the same way I did, but it didn't take long to find out that not everyone agreed. People believed what they wanted to believe and dismissed the rest.

I would have been fine with that, but the problem with that embracive way of thinking was that if you were wrong, the consequences were eternal. It is a flippant idea to think that everybody is right, and nobody is wrong – the Bible is just too specific to allow for such a lack of standards. The specter of Hell also raises the stakes somewhat.

But how does one determine who is right and who is mistaken? Do we flip a coin and hope for the best?

Obviously, human intelligence doesn't help, otherwise, we wouldn't have so many different beliefs. There are a lot of smart people out there who believe some pretty stupid things. Besides, since when is I.Q. a prerequisite for getting into Heaven? Do all the rest of us go to Hell just because we're dumb?

For years, I have maintained that there is a simple Litmus test that is the final witness to the Truth of God. It is the tangible presence of the Holy Spirit, or (as I would rather put it) the supernatural power of God. Simply put, you have to be able to feel His Spirit in order to be led by it.

The balance between right and wrong, between Heaven and Hell, is to walk that strait and narrow path that leads to Life. Only the Holy Spirit can give you the balance to do that. If you've got it, then you've got God; if you don't, you're on your own.

The Feast

"Ho, everyone that thirsteth, come ye to the waters..." Isaiah 55:1

The Book of John tells of one of the feasts that Jesus attended in Jerusalem where, at the conclusion of the feast, Jesus stood up and addressed the crowd with the same offer that Isaiah did. Here they were, surrounded with all sorts of food, drink, and an abundance of things to eat, and the Lord asked them if they were still hungry.

Are we still hungry today? We are surrounded by a multitude of religious food today. The airwaves are filled with a multitude of Christian broadcasters offering us their programs, tapes, books, and novelties – including little bottles of oil and rags to transfer a healing anointing for our infirmities. Christian bookstores are brimming with self-help books to lead us into a deeper and more fulfilling walk in God, and the Internet is packed with websites offering all that and much more.

Everywhere you turn, we are flooded with new programs to help us with everything from Bible study to riches to weight loss for Christ. It seems like everyone has a new, improved method. Maybe that's because the last ones didn't really work, and it's time for a new one.

And yet we are still waiting for a supernatural outpouring of the Holy Ghost.

Oh yes, I know it's coming. Haven't all our prophets of peace and prosperity told us that God wants to bless His children? We just have to buy a few more books and videos. Or perhaps we just haven't given enough money yet. Or maybe we just don't have enough faith. I'm sure there must be <u>some</u> reason.

Nevertheless, we are still left famished for something more than what we've filled our spiritual bellies with. Haggai puts it more succinctly. "Consider your ways," he tells us. You've eaten, but you're not filled. (Haggai 1:5)

When we consider our ways, do we snap ourselves out of our religious trance, or do we stand up from the table and realize that something is missing from the meal?

Could it be (perish the thought) that we are eating the wrong things? Perhaps the Bread of Life hasn't been served in our religious feasts. Maybe the Wine of God cannot be found poured out from our theological fountains. We are fat with "churchy" denominational platters piled high with all sorts of religious food, but the meal lacks the raw power of God, and so we keep eating, but we are not filled.

I love church. Most Christians do. Maybe that's because church is so easy. But do you hunger and thirst for something more?

There is a fountain of Living Waters that springs from the Throne of God that is the nectar of the saints. It alone can quench that thirst, but there is a price to pay to find it. You will have to seek the face of God.

Once you find it, it is offered freely, but it is not cheap. It was paid for by the Blood of Jesus Christ, and you can only get it from Him.

Decision

"A wise son heareth his father's instruction: but a scorner heareth not rebuke." Proverbs 13:1

I have noticed that whenever people gather together to make a compact with God to serve Him, there is always a time of testing and trial. How conflicting that must sound to an unbeliever, and yet it is the process in which God separates the wheat from the chaff.

Although history is full of examples, we as a people are often loath to believe that calamity will come upon us as long as we believe in God. Surely if we set our faces to serve the Lord, good things will happen – and they will. But before the blessings of God come, we face a bloody Cross that stands directly in our paths. It is at this point that decisions are made, and the true depth and intents of our hearts are exposed. Faith in God is measured not in the cadence and drumbeat as we begin our march but in the grit and determination to overcome the most severe obstacles that threaten to break us.

There are always tributary paths that seem like reasonable alternatives, even logical in contrast to the terrible costs that stand in the way which run alongside God's strait and narrow road, but they all lead off into slightly different destinations that may seem very similar to where the Lord is calling you, but without the severe price exacted of the Cross.

The ease of those paths seems to confirm their integrity, so we scorn those old paths that begin to seem senseless and destructive. But a wise son is defined by his fear of Almighty God, and although there are times when the path seems needlessly hard, he listens to his Father's instruction and presses on anyway. He overcomes, not because it makes sense, feels good, or has obvious advantages, but because it is the Truth, and that, more than anything, is what he is committed to.

Satan has his scorners to coax us on, while God has his prophets to warn us of our way. The funny thing is that, to those who choose the easy path, Satan's scorners seem like prophets, while God's prophets seem like scorners. Our hearts can so easily deceive us when we let them delude us.

And hence is the test of our lives – to yield to the transient or to pursue the ethereal. While the fruit of the former may be easily plucked and enjoyed, it is the latter that leads to the tree of Life.

As a nation which was founded upon the Gospel of Jesus Christ, I believe that we, will once more face a time of testing that will scrape the layers of rich, fertile earth that have covered our society and take us down to the bedrock of our souls. We will confront a time of hardship that will not seem fair, right, or good. It will be a time of decision.

It will also be the mercy of God.

> *"Multitudes, multitudes in the valley of decision: for the day of the LORD is near in the valley of decision." Joel 3:14*

Two Streams

"The way of a fool is right in his own eyes: but he that hearkeneth unto counsel is wise." Proverbs 12:15

To listen. That is one of the greatest gifts a person can have – the ability to listen to others. But human nature is such that when we lean more and more upon our own perspective, we lose that ability to see ourselves from other viewpoints.

Philosophy is full of witty sayings about walking in someone else's shoes. They are cute to quote but difficult to implement. I like the quip from Voltaire the best – "To know that you know what you know, and you don't know what you don't know is wisdom." Or in other words, stand on the principles you believe in but be humble enough to receive reproof. You just may be wrong about some things.

We are a fractious society. We all have our opinions and the freedom to express them, but you know what? Somebody's got to be wrong sometimes, and it just might be you, so it behooves us to learn how to listen to the old, time-tested words of the wise. We have a tendency to believe the things we want to believe, however, and we are loathe to relinquish them.

But that is not a formula for Truth.

I have watched the last couple of generations of American Christianity slowly evolve. Many of the strong beliefs that were so dearly held by the foundations of certain denominations have been replaced with newer, easier viewpoints. It has been like watching a river split into two different streams heading in basically the same direction, but with an ever-widening split between them.

The old-fashioned Gospel was strong in the belief of the chilling fear of God. Judgment and righteousness stood upon that foundation, and it led to a strong confidence in God and a separation from anything deemed worldly. God was in command, and as a result, the supernatural power and presence of the Holy Ghost was evident, even expected, in church services – something sorely missed today.

Something happened along the way, however, and we began to trickle away from the hard edge of righteousness. The fear of God began to be more of an idea of "reverence" rather than something worthy of "fear and trembling," and as the Love of God gained prominence, the Almighty Sovereign morphed into our "Daddy." Strict holiness and judgment became masked with a theme of "freedom in Christ," so naturally, we misinterpreted our emotional church celebrations to be outpourings of the Holy Spirit, not ever understanding the difference -- and the stream picked up speed and became a river.

As all rivers run, the small impressions in the landscape separating each stream soon become mountains. We can no longer see how far apart we have become because we can no longer see the other stream. And since our river is flowing along nicely, no one questions it anymore. Modern Christianity has become its own river with its own destination.

That would be fine if both streams ended up in the same place, but rivers rarely do.

The problem I see with increasing frequency is the inability of our modern church leadership to listen to the warnings coming from those on the other river. They can only hear the echoes of their own voices off the canyon walls that line the sides of their own river. Anything else is too faint to hear over the cacophony of the rush and turbulence of their own stream, and even if they could hear them, they are considered old-fashioned, narrow-minded, and out of touch with our modern society, and so sadly, they will not listen.

All truth is based on the Word of God, not traditions, interpretations, or new, modern ideas. When we blindly lean on our own viewpoints and refuse to listen to the old tried and true paths that we were once founded upon, we find ourselves rushing down a path that leads to a very different destination.

And it is very hard to paddle back upstream.

"Every way of a man is right in his own eyes: but the LORD pondereth the hearts." Proverbs 21:2

Butcher in Kenya

A pastor in Kenya told me something both exciting and funny that happened at one of his churches in Nairobi last week.

It seems that the wife of the Muslim Mahdi in town (the equivalent of an Islamic preacher) came to services for prayer for a cancerous growth on her shoulder. She had been given a short time to live and was in constant pain. She was desperate.

Now, understand that in Africa, it is no small thing for a Muslim to come to a Christian church, especially when you are the wife of the main Islamic preacher in town.

Well, Pastor John prayed over her, and sure enough, the Lord healed her right there on the spot -- the pain stopped immediately, and the growth disappeared. Needless to say, this amazed her and her family (including her husband), so she came back to the church with her children to thank the Christian pastor who had prayed for her. She and her children were so thankful that they accepted Jesus Christ as their Savior.

As she and her children were getting saved, the demonic spirits that were in them came out screaming. While we may not see much of that here in America, the demonic activity over there is so intense that you see this kind of thing often. I'll tell you, it's pretty freaky when you see it.

When they finished praying and received Jesus Christ into their hearts, the woman and her children got slain in the Spirit right there in the church, speaking in tongues.

Got the picture so far? Here you have the wife of a prominent Islam leader screaming and yelling as the demons are fleeing, and then lying there on the floor slain in the Spirit speaking in tongues.

Now, here's where the story picks up speed.

Because the noise could be heard all over the village, people were looking out their windows and doorways, wondering what all the commotion was. The local butcher also heard the noise and dropped what he was doing to rush out to find out what the problem was.

(A butcher in African society is considered an important personality in the village. This one also happened to be a Muslim at the local mosque.)

When he came running out of his shop, he forgot to leave his butcher knife behind, so now, EVERYBODY is paying attention as they're watching this Muslim butcher running, knife in hand, over to the church where the screaming was coming from.

As the butcher runs up to the door of the church, the power of the Holy Ghost crashed down on him also, and he was slain in the Spirit ... still holding his butcher knife! Immediately, Pastor John prayed over him and commanded the demonic spirits to come out of him and flee.

So now we have the Muslim preacher's wife and children on the floor praising Jesus and speaking in tongues, the members of the congregation running around with their hands raised in the air shouting praises to God ... and the butcher out cold in the doorway.

And they say God doesn't have a sense of humor!

When he came to, John took him through the Sinners Prayer (especially since he was still holding that meat cleaver), and the butcher became a Christian.

What a service! Ten souls got saved, and who knows how many more will come as a result of what happened. The Muslim preacher probably lost half his congregation that day, including his whole family, so it will be interesting to see what happens next.

Besides being an exciting and humorous story, I want to point out that this kind of power of God is exactly what we are missing in the church in America. We pride ourselves on being a Christian nation, but we can no longer point to the same manifestation of the power of the Holy Ghost anymore. We used to have this, but now it is rare at best. We've lost something holy and powerful in our transition to a sophisticated faith that no longer accepts the supernatural as something normal and expected. And yet, it is so common in third-world countries.

Shouldn't that tell us something? Could it be that perhaps we need to find a place of repentance before God and cry out to Him for forgiveness as a people who have gone astray and replaced faith with religion?

We jump up and down and sing songs, wave our hands in the air, and celebrate the love of Jesus, but we have left off to fear the Lord. As a result, we have become superficial in our faith and worship and are left listening to stories of how the power of God fell somewhere else to some other people far away.

The Old Prophet

> *"Howbeit the high places were not taken away: for as yet the people had not prepared their hearts unto the God of their fathers"* 2 Chronicles 20:33

Just the other day, I was asked a surprising question by an old prophet of God who had had a dramatic ministry throughout his life, filled with extraordinary moves of God, healings and miracles, and true revivals where thousands of souls were saved through his preaching. He wondered what happened to the outpourings of the Holy Spirit that had once been so common not that long ago.

Here was a man who knew what the power of God was like, and yet, no matter where he looked, that powerful manifestation of the Holy Spirit seemed to have evaporated from our religious landscape. The ministers of today that he has been speaking to never experienced first-hand what those old Holy Ghost services were like and, as a result, could never quite grasp what he was talking about.

Oh, sure, we've all heard the stories, but how many of us know what it is like to feel the pulsating charge of the Spirit of God as it lights up the entire church and lifts the congregation to another world? How many of us can testify to seeing the piles of discarded crutches left outside the tent revival's door? Where were we when, night after night, the altars were packed with lost souls crying out to God for Salvation, overwhelmed with the presence of the glory of God?

I had been part of that once, and so had he, but where could you go to find anything like that today? It has been so long since we've had that kind of outpouring that even our preachers have forgotten what it was like -- if they ever knew. What's worse, they have begun to think that the anemic church they now have is normal, and that what was experienced back then was abnormal.

Think I'm kidding? Just a few weeks ago, I listened to a guest preacher in an Assemblies of God church in Texas actually mock those old Holy Ghost preachers! How far have we come from what we once were!

The old prophet I spoke to had a hard time understanding how the church had fallen so far away in such a short time. The definition of the Fear of God has been watered down so much that it is now simply "reverence" and not the "fear and trembling" stuff that fueled those old brush arbor revivals.

Our church leaders have dismissed those who once stood in the awesome authority and power of God but instead have emphasized a new gospel of love and blessings, which is a lot more fun to listen to.

And we wonder what happened.

What will it take to get back to a time of miracles? What must we do in preparation for another move of God?

There are those who believe we will have a "breakthrough" if we sing songs and celebrate with praises, but those old-timers will tell you that there will be no revival without broken, repentant hearts and a willingness to crucify our ways to submit to holiness in the fear of God. They should know -- they had it; we don't.

But when will that happen?

As I look out, I see the same things Jehoshaphat saw – a people that have not prepared their hearts unto the God of their fathers and cannot see the difference.

Be sure, revival is coming just as it is written – just as soon as we repent and prepare our hearts to do it God's way.

About the Author

Dalen Garris has been in ministry since 1970 during the Jesus Movement in California. In 1997, he began a radio broadcast that ultimately spread to dozens of countries, from Israel and Saudi Arabia to Africa and the Philippines. His program, *Fire in the Hole*, was selected for broadcast four times a week for several years across North America on the Sky Angel network as the Voice of Jerusalem.

A newspaper column followed, for which he has written over 700 articles, which have been published in local newspapers and Christian magazines in several countries. He has also written over a dozen books and several booklets.

Since 2004, he has been lighting the fires of revival in churches spread across sub-Saharan Africa. During the course of 17 years, he has preached in over 1,000 churches and has seen hundreds of them set on fire and explode with growth, and hundreds of new ones planted across Africa. Hundreds of people have been supernaturally healed during the healing lines that so often sprang up during these revival meetings, and tens of thousands have been saved. And the fires are still burning.

Because of his work across Africa, Dalen Garris was awarded an honorary Doctorate in 2017 by the Northwestern Christian University of Florida.

Dr. Garris currently lives with Cindy, his wife of 43 years, in Waxahachie and is still heavily involved with churches across Africa. His pressing hope is to see this powerful move of God in Africa ignite us here in America. He believes that this upcoming generation will be the Gideon Generation that will usher in this last, great revival that he has preached about for so many years.

If you would like Dalen Garris to speak at your church or organization, please contact us for times and schedules.

Books by Dalen Garris:

Available at: www.Revivalfre.org/books

Four Steps to Revival
Do You Have Eternal Security?
Standing in the Gap
Two Covenants
Fire in the Hole

Revival Campaigns

The Kenya Diaries
A Trumpet in Nigeria
A Scent of Rain
Into the Heart of Darkness
Fire and Rain
Revival Campaigns in Africa – 2019
The Battle for Nigeria
A Light in the Bush
A Match in Dry Grass
Planting a Seed in Liberia
A Whisper in the Wind
Talking With the Women, by Cindy

A Voice in the Wilderness series:

vol. 1, The Journey Begins
vol. 2, the Early Years

vol. 3, Prophet Rising
vol. 4, Revival in the Wings
vol. 5, Sound of an Abundance of Rain
vol. 6, Watchman, What of the Night?
vol. 7, Mud and Heroes
vol. 8, Ashes in the Morning
vol. 9, Shaking the Olive Tree
vol. 10, Winds of Change
vol. 11, A Final Call

Booklets

Available at: www.Revivalfire.org/booklets/

A Volcano in Cape Verde

Tanzania, 2011

Nigeria, 2012

Calvinism Critiqued

When is the Rapture?

RevivalFire Ministries

PO Box 822, Waxahachie, TX 75168

dale@revivalfire.org

www.Revivalfire.org

www.ingramcontent.com/pod-product-compliance
Lightning Source LLC
Chambersburg PA
CBHW071513040426
42444CB00008B/1627